CATHOLICS, WAKE UP!
BE A SPIRITUAL WARRIOR

Jesse Romero

SERVANT
BOOKS

PUBLISHED BY FRANCISCAN MEDIA
Cincinnati, Ohio

Cover design by LUCAS Art & Design, Jenison, Michigan
Cover image © Masterfile
Book design by Mark Sullivan

LIBRARY OF CONGRESS CATALOGING-IN-PUBLICATION DATA
Romero, Jesse.
Catholics, wake up! : be a spiritual warrior / Jesse Romero.
pages cm
Includes bibliographical references and index.
ISBN 978-1-61636-816-6 (alk. paper)
1. Christian life—Catholic authors. I. Title.
BX2350.3.R657 2014
248.4'82--dc23
2014030166

ISBN 978-1-61636-816-6

Published by Servant Books, an imprint of Franciscan Media
28 W. Liberty St.
Cincinnati, OH 45202
www.FranciscanMedia.org

Printed in the United States of America.
Printed on acid-free paper.
15 16 17 18 5 4 3

CONTENTS

Today, many Catholics believe that the Catholic faith is like a club where you can pick and choose which beliefs you like and discard those you dislike. However, the Catholic Church is certainly not a club—it is the living body of Jesus Christ! It is an encounter with the God of the universe who reveals himself through his body, the Church.

It was Jesus who founded the Church, and he promised that the gates of hell would not prevail against it. We must never forget that Catholicism is based on *revelation*, meaning to "tear down the veil." That means that God tells us who he is—we do not tell him who we think he is! We read in Matthew's Gospel:

> [Jesus] asked his disciples, "Who do men say that the Son of man is?" And they said, "Some say John the Baptist, others say Elijah, and others Jeremiah or one of the prophets." He said to them, "But who do you say that I am?" Simon Peter replied, "You are the Christ, the Son of the living God." And Jesus answered him, "Blessed are you, Simon Bar-Jonah. For flesh and blood has not revealed this to you, but my Father who is in heaven." (Matthew 16:13–17)

This is what we mean by revelation! You do not take a *Time* magazine or *Newsweek* poll to find out who God is; God tells us himself! It was the same two thousand years ago when people thought Jesus was John the Baptist or Elijah. Only God can tell us who he is, period. We either accept it or reject it—we do not create him in *our* image. You may be familiar with the old adage, attributed to Voltaire, that says: "God created man in his own image, and man returned the favor."

On October 11, 1992, in his apostolic constitution *Fidei Depositum,* Pope John Paul II opened with this line: "Guarding the deposit of the faith is the mission entrusted by Christ to His Church." The purpose of the Church is to guard what God revealed to us in the person of Jesus Christ! This is *the* Church's mission! We cannot change what has been revealed; we can only accept it or reject it.

Too often people ask when the Church is going to get caught up with the times. The answer must be "Never!" if the Church is going to stay faithful to her Founder! The Church is called to reach out anew in every time and culture, but the Church cannot change the Truth. The Church can repackage the truth in new and varied ways, but the essential content will not change. Many people don't want to hear this because they want the Church to agree with them and *their* views. But that would make the Church a mere culture club that wants to be accepted by everyone and is eager to please people in order to get many members.

With all this in mind, Jesse Romero wrote this book as a true wake-up call for all Catholics. I encourage you to read this book with a mind that is open and eager for the truth. Sometimes Jesse might make you mad by the way he says things—good! This will motivate you to deal with what he is saying, struggle with it, pray about it, and ask God himself to reveal the truth to you.

Jesse throws out a challenge for Catholics to stop sitting on the sidelines and instead get involved in the living reality of their faith. Today the Church needs men and women who will witness to the truth of Jesus and his Church by the way they think, live, and believe. We have to first encounter the truth in the person of Jesus Christ, and then we need to get busy evangelizing to bring others into this truth.

The great news is that we do not have to evangelize others by arguing with them or trying to convince them that we are right and they are wrong if we do it effectively through the Holy Spirit. Jesus promised us: "You shall receive power when the Holy Spirit has come upon you; and you shall be my witnesses" (Acts 1:8). God loves every person and "desires all men to be saved and to come to knowledge of the truth" (1 Timothy 2:4). God calls us to be his instruments of salvation, if only we will get out of the way and let him use us to bring others to him. We cannot not say, "Let the priests and bishops do it." We cannot say, "Let Jesse Romero do it." What we need to say is, "*I* want to do it!" Jesus himself said "Go therefore and make disciples of all nations" (Matthew 28:19). This is not a suggestion; it is a command, and this book will help you live this command! Do not be afraid—God is with you!

—Fr. Larry Richards, author of *The Full Armor of God*

CHAPTER ONE

From Martial Arts to the Art of Souls

For to me to live is Christ.
—Philippians 1:21

I have been Catholic all my life, but it was really just part of my Latino cultural tradition. In my heart, I did not love God. How could I? I hardly knew him. I lived the first twenty-five years of my life in a secular coma. Faith, religion, God, death, judgment, heaven, and hell never really entered my mind. Ephesians 5:14 describes what I experienced: "Awake, O sleeper, and arise from the dead, and Christ shall give you light."

Essentially, there are four types of Catholics: cultural (or cradle) Catholics; traditional Catholics; cafeteria Catholics; and evangelical Catholics. Let's look at the characteristics of each of these.

Cultural Catholics. If you are a cradle (or cultural) Catholic, your parents baptized you as an infant, you go to Mass every Sunday, and you probably go to Catholic School or at least take religious instruction. It's an external type of Catholicism, though; you don't really know how to explain or defend the faith.

Traditional Catholics. My parents are a good example of traditional Catholics. Born in Mexico and raised with very little education, Catholicism was in their DNA. They live out the devotions of the Church; they are pious, prayerful, and humble. They have a deep-rooted faith, but it's very personal—so personal that they are reticent to share their faith, in part because they have never been taught how to articulate it.

Cafeteria Catholics. These Catholics pick and choose what they want to believe. They might be angry with the Church because it's not progressive enough for them. They question the Church's authority and want things to change.

Evangelical Catholics. These are Catholics who have fallen in love with Jesus. They know their faith, live in a state of grace, love the Bible, honor Our Lady, are faithful to the magisterium of the Church, and actively share and defend their faith.

I was raised in a traditional Catholic family. I attended Catholic schools, and we went to Mass every Sunday as a family. We also prayed the rosary at least once a week as a family. As far as I can remember my parents were active in the Church. My father had a conversion experience through a Cursillo retreat, after which he traded the life of a functional alcoholic for the life of a sober man of God. My mother was born with the gift of deep abiding faith. I saw many nights when my mother would be praying trains of rosaries and litanies for my father who was at the local bar drinking and gambling until the late morning hours.

In my formative years I was clearly sheltered in a Catholic culture, and as a kid I thought the whole world was Catholic. I basically lived in a Catholic barrio; everything in our family life and neighborhood revolved around our local Catholic parish.

From Cultural Catholic to Secular Humanist

In my teen years, I became addicted to both the martial arts and the Chicano civil rights movement that permeated the barrios in the 1970s. These two influences overshadowed virtually all the Catholic Christian beliefs that had been instilled in me. The crisis of faith I experienced is but a microcosm of what happens in the life of the typical Southern California Latino youth. Like so many of them, I became a pragmatic atheist in my teens; I had Catholic sensibilities and sentiments, but I had a secular humanist mindset.

When secular humanism grabbed hold of me, I became infected by the slick-talking, politically correct experts of this world. I had descended from "cultural Catholicism" to "cafeteria Catholicism." Being in this condition is like stumbling along in the dark, not even aware that it *is* dark. I lived in this comatose spiritual condition for many years, although I still attended Mass (more out of trying to keep harmony with my parents than conviction). I never even questioned the Catholic Faith as I was growing up because I was indifferent and apathetic towards religion.

From the age of thirteen to eighteen, I became immersed in the martial arts. There is no doubt that the martial arts harnessed my energy in the right direction, and it probably kept me from a life of juvenile delinquency. I idolized the martial arts superstars, with Bruce Lee at the top of my list. I was awarded my black belt at the age of eighteen in Tang Soo Do Korean karate. Then I became a second-generation Chuck Norris black belt. While I attended junior college, I worked at a supermarket and I began teaching karate. At this stage in my life, I thought about God only on occasions, particularly at funerals and weddings. The things of God just didn't factor into my secular humanist mind. More than anything else, I was guided by my concupiscence: the lust of the flesh, the lust of the eyes, and the pride of life. My god was an unholy trinity called me, myself, and I.

At the age of twenty-one, I joined the Los Angeles Sheriff's Department. That same year I got married to my wife, Anita. My parents were happy—they had always admonished me to marry a Catholic from my own Latino culture. My wife was a cultural Catholic, devoted to her faith but just as unformed as I was.

Being a deputy sheriff at the age of twenty-one, with all the authority vested in me by the state of California, made me somewhat arrogant, prideful, and self-righteous. While I was going through the Academy, I was well respected among the other cadets for my physical fitness and my martial arts background. I hung out with all the other "jocks" (physically fit cadets), and we would haze the less physically fit, more "nerdy" cadets. There was one cadet who I liked to harass because I saw him as a "softie"—he was uncoordinated and not very physically fit. I believed that "might makes right" and "only the strong survive," in addition to being full of a lot of "Chicano power rage." I was driven to train myself mentally and physically to have a fighting spirit and to become a deadly weapon.

Upon graduation from the Academy, this cadet whom I considered a softie gave me a wrapped gift. He wished me well, said that he had enjoyed our friendship, and concluded by saying, "God bless you." I was stunned. Here was a guy who had every reason in the world to dislike me, yet he gave me a gift and imparted a blessing to me. This type of overt Christian behavior had an effect on my secular mind; I couldn't wrap my mind around a random act of kindness in public. It was a moment of grace for me.

I went home, opened the gift, and lo and behold, it was a *Catholic Living Bible*. I said to myself, "What kind of person would do something like this after being treated so badly?" I put the Bible on the coffee table and promised myself that I would read it daily, because I was genuinely curious to read all it had to say; I knew there was something unique about the Bible. Well, just as in the parable of the sower where the seed falls among thorns, I was like the one who hears the Word but then worldly anxiety and the lure of riches choke the Word and it bears no fruit. I relegated my Bible to the coffee table for the next couple of years. It sat there, lifeless, pages stuck together, spine intact, still in the cellophane wrapper. My version of "Bible-thumping" was on Fridays when I would dust the furniture and dust off my Bible.

My job was really changing me for the worst; I was young and impressionable, working in the Los Angeles County Men's Central Jail, considered to be one of the largest jails in the world and full of violence. As I walked into that jail every day, even I could feel the strong presence of evil. At this point in my young life, I did not have a strong moral conscience. I witnessed many deputies who coped with the stress of the job by turning to alcohol, gambling, and sexual immorality. Law enforcement has one of the highest rates of divorce and depression as compared to other occupations. My priorities were my career, karate, and another newly discovered passion, competitive amateur boxing.

A Different Path

In the midst of this aggressive, violent, competitive, secular world, full of testosterone, the Lord sent me a breath of fresh air. I met a deputy sheriff named Paul Clay. He definitely marched to a different drummer. He had a genuine love for people and there was a sense of peace about him that I couldn't understand. He was also full of joy, which bugged me; I used to tell Paul that once he put on his sheriff's uniform, he needed to get rid of that happy-go-lucky attitude. He would just chuckle. I am sure he pitied my secular way of thinking.

Working side by side in Los Angeles, we developed a very deep friendship. We would work out every day together—we would go running or lift weights—and all the while he would talk to me about Jesus Christ. He quoted the Bible with such familiarity that I was mesmerized by the wisdom that flowed from his words. His behavior, his vocabulary, and his family life were also consistent with his love for God.

Paul would ask me questions about my Catholic faith, but I had no answers. He would ask me if I had accepted the Lord. Where would I spend eternity if I died tonight? Was I saved? Was I born again? Did I have an assurance of my salvation? These questions seemed a little strange to me. I didn't remember such questions from my *Baltimore Catechism* days. However, these questions were scratching me where I itched, both intellectually and spiritually.

I started taking a spiritual inventory of my life. I came to the honest conclusion that I knew *about* Jesus, I had heard stories about him, but I didn't *know* Jesus as the Lord of my life. I had never appropriated the faith of my childhood; I had never made a personal, sincere declaration of faith in Jesus Christ of my own volition. I had prayed a lot of words during Holy Mass but I did so without any love; it was just to fulfill an obligation. I came to the startling conclusion that I was spiritually bankrupt.

I was a perfectionist in everything I endeavored to do, whether it was sports, school, or career. I always wanted to be at the top of my game, and I suddenly realized that I was not prepared for the last four things at the end of my earthly existence: death, judgment, heaven, and hell. My moral conscience spoke loudly to me: "Knowing Jesus is a matter of life and death," and in this area I was failing miserably. The words of sacred Scripture came into my heart like a bolt of lightning: "For what will it profit a man, if he gain the whole world, and forfeits his life?" (Matthew 16:26).

Paul gave me a Christian tract that said if you are not moving forward spiritually, you are probably moving backward. The world had taught me that he who dies with the most toys wins, but this tract said that he who dies with forgiveness of sins wins. This now totally made sense to me. All the sacramental graces I had received throughout the course of my life were stirring within my soul.

Paul and I had been engaging in spiritual dialogue for a couple of months, and he had given me many non-Catholic Christian books, tapes, and tracts. One evening after work as we walked to our cars in the employee parking lot, Paul asked me, "Had you ever made a personal commitment to Jesus?" He told me that I could not be saved through the faith of my parents or a priest; I had to take my own step of faith and invite the Lord into my heart and life personally. I answered him honestly that I hadn't made that personal commitment, and he responded by telling me that's what was missing in my life. The he told me something I will never forget: "Most people will miss heaven by about twelve inches." When I asked him what he meant, he said the distance between the head and the heart is about twelve inches, and true faith must travel from the head to the heart. That hit me like a ton of bricks. Paul had a lot of credibility with me, because I saw love in his heart for everyone.

From Head to Heart

I drove home after that conversation with Paul realizing that I had a fair amount of head knowledge about Jesus but my heart was empty. I began crying as I drove down the interstate. I realized that I had endeared my heart to worldly things that really didn't matter in the grand scheme of life. My addictions and enslavements to creature comforts would not matter when I crossed the threshold of eternity.

When I arrived home, I knelt down in my living room and I looked at a picture of the Sacred Heart of Jesus that was given to me by my parents. I felt the unspeakably warm presence of Jesus in such a powerful way that night. I remember my parents telling me that wherever the Sacred Heart of Jesus is honored, he will bless that household. I pulled out a tract that Paul had given me about "the four spiritual laws," and I sincerely prayed the "Sinner's Prayer" on the back of the card. That day Jesus Christ became real to me.

This mystical encounter was a pivotal conversion point in my life. In an instant, the current of my life was altered, and I believed in Jesus with such force and tenacity, with such an uprising of my whole being, with a conviction so powerful, with such a certainty that leaves no sort of doubt. Since then, all the hazards of a constantly changing world have not been able to dilute my remembrance of this profound revelation. This conversion to the lordship of Jesus Christ occurred in 1988. My conversion was not simply some emotional encounter, either. There was a rush of reason, and the assurance that Jesus was the Son of God who *rose from the dead* flooded my soul. That night I felt as if I had reached back two thousand years, grabbed hold of the cross, and let the blood of Jesus wash me clean.

The Holy Bible immediately became like a love letter to me from God; it became like a window out of this prison-like world through which I could look at eternity and be refreshed. I began listening to all the tapes and reading all the books and pamphlets Paul had given me. I read large sections of the Bible daily; the person of Jesus Christ came right out of the printed pages of Scripture and became a reality. I especially started immersing myself in the Gospels night after night. I listened to all the radio preachers Paul recommended, especially the *Bible Answer Man* radio program. I began attending Protestant events, concerts, and services on my own because I wanted to find out the truth, the whole truth and nothing but the truth about the Lord Jesus Christ. I promised the Lord that I would follow him wherever he led me.

I found out that Paul was a fallen-away Catholic who identified himself as a non-denominational (fundamentalist) Christian.

He seemed very sure of himself when he shared his faith with me, and I took it all in like a sponge. Not being anchored well to the Catholic Faith, I saturated myself in the world of evangelical fundamentalism. Every waking moment found me listening to a different radio preacher and following along in my Bible. I heard significant amounts of anti-Catholic propaganda, and I began to believe it, since I had never heard a Catholic answer to refute these charges. After a good solid year of this indoctrination, I was convinced that the Catholic religion was "unbiblical" and leading people into error.

I gave my testimony at a small fundamentalist church that Paul attended. My wife knew all that was going on in my life spiritually, and she saw that my Catholicism was hanging by a thread. Some Protestant preachers said that the Catholic Church was a cult, while others taught that it was Christian but had some errors. Through Protestant fundamentalism I learned about the Holy Trinity, the deity of Christ, the virgin birth, the bodily resurrection, the blood atonement, and the inerrancy of Scripture. I shared what I was learning with my parents one day, and they were surprised that I thought this was novel. My parents told me those six fundamental truths are historic Catholic truths. That conversation opened my mind towards the possibility that some Catholics might be "Christian" and may be "saved."

Catholic vs. Protestant

My wife recognized that I was undergoing a spiritual odyssey. She was conflicted, happy, and worried all at the same time. My wife was content being a cultural Catholic. She knew I was church shopping and visiting other Protestant church services. She sat down with me one day and told me that she liked the positive changes that she saw in me, but she wasn't sure she was going to like the ending. My wife had no interest in leaving the Catholic Church. I quickly pointed out to her with my newly acquired biblical repertoire, "Honey, the Bible says, 'Wives submit yourself to your husbands.'" The arrogant manner with which I said this quickly ended that conversation. (Of course, I didn't read the entire passage that also says, "Husbands, love your wives just as Christ loves the Church.")

We talked the next day when both of us were calm, and my wife affirmed the good qualities that she saw in me which were virtuous. However, she added that if I left the Catholic Church, this would disrupt our marriage because she wasn't going to leave the Catholic Church. I then let the cat out of the bag by telling her I believed that the Catholic Church taught error based on all the reading I had done, the tapes I had listened to, and the radio preachers who were teaching me biblical truth.

My wife challenged me; she threw down the gauntlet. She said, "Before you run off to some other church—or worse yet, start your own—why don't you study Catholicism from Catholic sources? You have had your nose studiously in non-Catholic Christian litera-ture for the past year and a half. If you can prove to yourself that Catholicism is wrong from Catholic sources, then I will respect you if you still want to leave. But first give it a chance."

Being a deputy sheriff, I saw great validity to her argument. After all, I knew that hearsay testimony is inadmissible in a court of law, and all my anti-Catholic biases were hearsay; I had never investigated Catholicism from Catholic sources. Bishop Fulton Sheen once said: "There are not a hundred people in America who hate the Catholic Church. There are millions of people who hate what they wrongly believe to be the Catholic Church—which is, of course, quite a different thing."[1]

I accepted my wife's challenge, especially since I saw the prospect of her leaving the Catholic Church with me if I proved that Catholicism was wrong. I told her very confidently, "Honey, this is going to be easy because there are *no* Catholic answers to my objections." I went on to assure my wife that Catholicism is an aberration of the true Gospel.

My wife told my parents that I was shopping around at non-Catholic churches. My parents affirmed that they were proud that I had experienced a conversion to the Lordship of Jesus Christ, and they told me they understood my feelings and emotions (unbeknownst to me they had become involved in the Catholic Charismatic Renewal). My parents had always been authentically devout Catholics, but now they were reading Sacred Scripture daily and were heavily involved in Catholic evangelization. My parents invited my wife and I to attend the "Encuentro Latino," a massive Hispanic Catholic Charismatic conference, where they said I would meet other Catholics who love the Scriptures, had a relationship with Jesus Christ, believed in evangelization, and were faithful to the Catholic Church.

The Los Angeles Sports Arena was packed: more than twenty thousand Catholics praising the Lord in song and sharing powerful Christ-centered conversion testimonies. We witnessed Catholic clergy and laypeople giving dynamic, Bible-based evangelistic preaching, and we attended Eucharistic Adoration and reverent sacred liturgies. At one point, one of the priests had all of us get on our knees while the Eucharistic Lord was exposed in the monstrance, and he led us in a prayer to dedicate or rededicate our lives to Jesus Christ. This was a powerful moment of grace for me; there was a thick cloud of holiness that descended over the crowd. There were people claiming to be healed of all kinds of illnesses and delivered from demonic contamination.

I definitely felt at home at this conference, even though I still had doctrinal questions about Catholicism. I was overcome by the emotional experience of being in the presence of God; I felt his presence like never before. I decided to put all my doctrinal questions on hold for a while as I enjoyed this "honeymoon" experience with the Lord. My wife also experienced a great spiritual awakening that weekend, and we both became involved with the Catholic Charismatic Renewal.

We began attending conferences, workshops, Life in the Spirit seminars, healing Masses, praise gatherings, prayer meetings and evangelization retreats. We were totally committed as a Catholic couple. We went to a Marriage Encounter, and the Lord blessed us with our first child. We named him Paul, after my favorite apostle and my friend who had introduced me to the lordship of Jesus Christ.

After a while, the honeymoon phase of my conversion was over, and now I wanted answers to some of my questions about Catholicism. I wanted to know what I believed and why I believed it, and I wanted to be sure Catholicism could be reconciled with the Holy Bible. Fundamentalist Christianity had left me with a residue of anti-Catholicism. At this point I had a Catholic heart but a Protestant mind, theology, and vocabulary. I met with my parents' parish priest, and he acknowledged that I had a lot of good questions. He offered to send me to a Catholic Answers conference entitled "Go Forth and Teach," which would be held at the Long Beach Marriot. He told me that Catholic Answers was a lay apostolate founded by Catholic apologists who were experts at answering Protestant objections and misunderstandings.

I attended this conference with two other parishioners, and we were encouraged to ask the presenters all the tough questions we had and thoroughly pick their brains. This seminar was three days long, but it seemed like twenty minutes. The cadre of speakers included Karl Keating, Patrick Madrid, Mark Brumley, Scott Hahn, Thomas Howard, Deal Hudson, and Fr. Mitch Pacwa. For me, the weekend was like a spiritual boot camp—thirty hours of high-powered evangelization and high-octane apologetics. All my Protestant objections came crumbling down like a house of cards. All of my objections, questions, doubts, and insecurities received compelling, cogent, biblical, and historical Catholic answers. The Catholic faith came to life for me—right from the pages of my NIV Protestant Bible!

I thought to myself, *Why wasn't I taught this before? Why didn't I know this? Why wasn't I given good Catholic apologetics in all of my years of Catholic school?* I thought about the thousands of Catholics who have left the true Church of Christ for denominational Christianity (like my friend Paul), who never knew what they left. They were never catechized, nor were they ever given good, biblical, Catholic answers to their questions. Watered-down Catholicism doesn't attract anyone, but unadulterated Catholicism is like a divine magnet; it is addictive.

The conference that weekend injected me with spiritual steroids. It overhauled my Catholic faith and education big time. I was literally surprised by truth (the title of one of the many apologetics books I purchased years later). I felt truly born again after this apologetics conference—no more confusion, no more searching. I went home, burst through the front door, and embraced my wife, Anita. I cried and repented for trying to take her out of the Catholic Church. I repented for having slandered and spoken falsely about the true Church of Jesus Christ. We wept in each other's arms.

We truly became a Catholic Christian couple that day; we were both flooded with God's grace. As a couple, we were fully submitted to the lordship of Jesus Christ; we honored Our Lady, were obedient to the Church, loved the Scriptures, and were committed to evangelism. I made a vow to my wife and to the Lord that I would serve the Catholic Church for the rest of my life with the same fighting spirit that catapulted me to the status of U.S.A. national kickboxing champion and three-time World Police Olympic middleweight boxing champion.

Ever since that day back in 1990, I've lived my life with a sense of urgency to evangelize. As Pope John Paul II says, "It is not enough to discover Christ—you must bring him to others."[2] To reach people with the lifesaving message of the Gospel means that we have to walk it, talk it, preach it, pray it, rap it, teach it, tell it, write it, type it, live it, give it, wear it, share it, shout it, sing it, scream it, proclaim it—we must live for Jesus. Evangelism is not something we do; it is who we are. I came across the following declaration of what it means to make a decision for Christ, and I refer to it often.

THE FELLOWSHIP OF THE UNASHAMED

I'm part of the Fellowship of the Unashamed. The die has been cast. I have stepped over the line. The decision has been made. I'm a disciple of Christ, and I won't look back, let up, slow down, back away, or be still.

My past is redeemed. My present makes sense. My future is secure. I'm finished with low living, sight walking, small planning, smooth knees, colorless dreams, tamed visions, mundane talking, cheap living, and dwarfed goals.

I no longer need preeminence, lavish wealth, position, promotions, plaudits, or popularity. I don't have to be right, or first, or tops, or recognized, or praised, or rewarded. I live by faith, lean on His presence, walk by patience, lift by prayer, and labor by the Holy Spirit's power.

My face is set. My gait is fast. My goal is Heaven. My road may be narrow, my way rough, my companions few, but my Guide is reliable and my mission is clear.

I will not be bought, compromised, detoured, lured away, turned back, deluded, or delayed.

I will not flinch in the face of sacrifice or hesitate in the presence of the adversary. I will not negotiate at the table of the enemy, ponder at the pool of popularity, or meander in the maze of mediocrity.

I won't give up, shut up, or let up until I have stayed up, stored up, prayed up, paid up, and preached up for the cause of Christ.

I am a disciple of Jesus. I must give until I drop, preach until all know, and work until He comes. And when He does come for His own, He'll have no problems recognizing me. I am part of the Fellowship of the Unashamed.[3]

The Journey from Darkness to Light

I was actually instructed *against* the Church's moral teachings on several occasions. One priest threw my *Catechism* across the room when I asked him questions about contraception in paragraphs 2399 and 2370. He became angry that I brought up the subject to several people at the parish during a small group gathering.

Another priest took my copy of the *Humane Vitae* encyclical out of my hand and threw it in the trash. He admonished me never to bring this document to the parish again, and he ordered me not to discuss this subject with anybody in the parish. As the pastor, he said he was the final authority on these matters and the Church's teaching. He told me that he had a doctorate from Berkeley and did not agree with *Humane Vitae*.

Yet another priest—the one that actually performed our wedding ceremony—told my wife and me plainly, without batting an eye: "What birth control are you going to use? I usually recommend the pill to all the couples I am going to marry." (As a sad postscript, this priest eventually was arrested for sex crimes and was sent to prison.) I pray for his conversion and that of many other priests who poorly catechized my generation.

When I got married, I had no intention of having children; in fact, I stated that to my wife many times. I wanted to be a married single; I wanted to indulge in sports, exercise, vacations, surplus income, and all the other commodities of life. My mind was jaded and I was a total pessimist from what I had seen as a young L.A. deputy sheriff and from growing up in a barrio replete with gangs, drugs, violence, and sexual promiscuity. I would often say to my wife, "There is no way I want to bring a baby into this filthy, violent, corrupt society." My wife would just sigh in response, sadly realizing she had married someone who didn't mean the vows I professed at the altar.

I never saw myself being a father. I wanted my wife and I to be like the educated, professional, self-indulgent couple depicted in the media that looked so happy and enjoyed sex anytime without any consequences. I never intended to have kids, and I told my wife on countless occasions that she had better take the pill because if she got pregnant I would walk out on her. My wife actually had an excellent case for an annulment, yet she put up with my immaturity. She sought refuge with my mother, and together they simply stormed the gates of heaven for years praying for my conversion.

To say that my mind was corrupt was to put it mildly. At this stage in my life, Jesus Christ was not the center of my life; he was in the sidelines somewhere. The Scripture identified the condition of my soul accurately: "For although they knew God they did not honor him as God or give thanks to him, but they became futile in their thinking and their senseless minds were darkened" (Romans 1:21).

After coming wholeheartedly back to the Catholic faith, I heard Scott Hahn mention a book on contraception. I ordered this book and read it from cover to cover. Next my wife and I signed up for a class on Natural Family Planning at a neighboring parish. Our souls were flooded with light. My wife went to our bathroom medicine cabinet, looked at the birth control pills with contempt, and threw them all out. As I watched in silence, she turned to me and said, "I had a feeling it was wrong, but now that I know it's wrong—never, ever again. From now on, we will do what the Church teaches."

I believe that my story is but a microcosm of millions of other Catholics who have been poorly catechized. Many have been stumbling along in the dark and not even realizing that it is dark. Many are starving, yet not even realize they are hungry (for truth).

The Tsunami of Secularism

To say that we are facing a difficult challenge as Christians today is putting it mildly. We are being confronted with the fight of our life. The generations that will follow are depending on us now, today, to do what is necessary to fight for and preserve the truth. They are depending on the training we provide for them, and we are all called by God to engage in that training. No one who truly believes in Jesus Christ can sit this one out.

During a press conference on October 8, 2012, Cardinal Wuerl said that the current crisis of faith could be attributed to a "tsunami of secular influence that has swept across the cultural landscape."[4] We all need to respond to this tsunami with holy zeal and a fighting spirit, otherwise we run a great risk of being consumed by it. Many more lives will experience unnecessary chaos if we sit back and do nothing. Let's work together in whatever ways we can to train up the hearts, minds and souls of the future generations! We must be battle-ready—even the power of a tsunami can never wash away the love of God!

For Reflection

1. If you were raised in the Church, how would you describe your Catholic upbringing? Which of the four types of Catholics are you?

2. How do you feel about the statement, "From now on, we will do what the Church teaches"? Are there any areas in your life that might need to change?

3. What can you do where you live and work to counter the secularism that continues to gain hold?

CHAPTER TWO

The Catholic Evangelist

Always be steady, endure suffering,
do the work of an evangelist,
fulfil your ministry.
—2 Timothy 4:5

How would you define *Catholic evangelization*? Like many Catholics today, you might shy away from this term, imagining it to be way out of your comfort zones. Maybe you think these two words just don't belong together—that evangelization is better left to fundamentalist preachers. But my definition of Catholic evangelization is very simple: helping others to love God, saving souls, and slaying error. Catholic evangelists are those that "have their own part to play in the mission of the whole Christian people in the Church and in the world" (*CCC* 897).

We are all sent to evangelize a lost and fallen world and do combat against the culture of death. The Church needs laypeople in all walks of life: actors, politicians, teachers, doctors, professional athletes, blue-collar workers, police officers, mail carriers, hairstylists, business owners, and parents. Through receiving the Eucharist, we are strengthened and equipped to go out and evangelize a secular world. The *Catechism* goes on to say:

> By reason of their special vocation it belongs to the laity to seek the kingdom of God by engaging in temporal affairs and directing them according to God's will…. It pertains to

them in a special way so to illuminate and order all temporal things with which they are closely associated that these may always be affected and grow according to Christ and maybe to the glory of the Creator and Redeemer. (*CCC* 898)

I owned a boxing gym that I operated for several years back in the nineties in East Los Angeles. I ran my gym by a code of strict discipline. I didn't allow any cursing or profanities, and I hung a big crucifix in the middle of the gym, where it was prominently displayed. When I was training my boxers, I would shout instructions (much like a military drill instructor) to keep them motivated and inspired. And guess what? My boxers most enjoyed when I would shout out inspirational Bible verses during their arduous training sessions! Some of their favorites were:

Blessed be the Lord, my rock,
    who trains my hands for war,
        and my fingers for battle. (Psalm 144:1)

What then shall we say to this? IF God is for us, who is against us? (Romans 8:31)

Fight the good fight of the faith. (1 Timothy 6:12)

I can do all things in [Christ] who strengthens me.
(Philippians 4:13)

Characteristics of an Effective Evangelist

Even though the term *evangelist* doesn't sound very Catholic to most of us, evangelizing is a big part of being a spiritual warrior. After all, Catholics were the original evangelizers—they are the reason Christianity exists.

Evangelization requires on-the-job training. You get better as you do it, but you only learn by doing. We're called to "grow in the grace and knowledge of our Lord and Savior Jesus Christ" (2 Peter 3:18). We will make mistakes; we cannot expect to know the answer to every question or be absolutely positive that we are using the best possible approach to help a particular person to know Jesus Christ and his Church. Some people have the gift of gab, and this helps, but the single most important characteristic of a successful evangelizer is not intelligence, or training, or courage, or even self-confidence—it's *holiness*. As 1 Thessalonians 4:3 says, "This is the will of God, your sanctification"(*NAB*).

The *Catechism* tells us that "the initiative of lay Christians is necessary especially when the matter involves discovering or inventing the means for permeating social, political, and economic realities with the demands of Christian doctrine and life," and it goes on to say that "lay believers are in the front line of Church life" (*CCC* 899). We should use whatever means we can to permeate our culture. This includes radio, television, social media, and being involved in our local neighborhoods and communities. All of these provide many opportunities to evangelize, catechize, inspire, and help form the moral conscience of those around us. We can also be an example to the "low-information" Catholics around us, inspiring them to wake up and become warriors in their own spheres of influence.

> Lay Christians...have the right and duty, individually or grouped in associations, to work so that the divine message of salvation may be known and accepted by all men throughout the earth. (*CCC* 900)

If you feel like you don't have the training or authority to evangelize, remember that your baptism and confirmation has given you not only the authority, but the right and duty to do so.

Evangelization and Worship Go Hand in Hand

During slow weeknights when I worked patrol in the Los Angeles Sheriff's Department, I would take the microphone and drive to neighborhoods infested with gangs. I was a rebel with a cause. My cause was to win back souls for Christ.

You can use whatever means at your disposal to reach souls. Your daily work, your prayers, your family life, recreational activity all can become spiritual sacrifices and ways to influence the world for Christ. And while you are living your life this way, you are also offering worship! The *Catechism* teaches us that we worship "everywhere by [our] holy actions" and thus "consecrate the world itself to God, everywhere offering worship by the holiness of [our] lives" (*CCC* 901).

Twelve Jewish men who followed Jesus changed the world with their witness, their testimony, and their love for truth. The Bible says the apostles "turned the world upside down" (Acts 17:6). We, too, are meant to turn our world upside down. We're not meant to float along like bumps on a log, going with the flow and not making waves. We're meant to upset the status quo!

The first place we do this is in our families. Parents, after all, are the first and foremost evangelizers of their children. This is an important task that can't be relegated to others. Sending your children to religious education classes—or even to a Catholic school—can't take the place of teaching your children day by day what it means to honor

God, live a life of virtue and holiness, and serve others. Remember, you're raising your own army of kingdom warriors!

> By the sacrament of confirmation, [the baptized] are more perfectly bound to the Church and are enriched with a special strength of the Holy Spirit. Hence they are, as true witnesses of Christ, more strictly obliged to spread and defend the faith by word and deed. (*CCC* 1285)

When your children receive the sacrament of confirmation, they are charged with both spreading and defending the faith—by their words and by their actions. They aren't too young to be evangelists; this is a lifelong calling.

How many of us, even as adults, feel adequate for this task? If we don't, we can actively seek out formation in this area so we are always "prepared to make a defense to any one who calls you to account for the hope that is in you" (1 Peter 3:15).

Young or old, we all should be dedicated to the work of evangelization—preaching and teaching the Catholic faith so as to seek out the lost and make known to all men the love and salvation of Jesus Christ. "I will seek the lost, and I will bring back the strayed" (Ezekiel 34:16).

For Reflection

1. What comes to mind when you hear the word evangelist?
2. How do you see yourself engaging the culture and taking your place on the front lines in the war on souls?
3. If you are a parent, what can you do to actively train your children so they are confident speaking about their faith? If you're not a parent, how can you become more confident yourself when someone questions your faith?

CHAPTER THREE

I Don't Have Enough Faith to Be an Atheist

> For what can be known about God is plain to them because God has shown it to them. Ever since the creation of the world his invisible nature, namely, his eternal power and deity, has been clearly perceived in the things that have been made.
>
> —Romans 1:19–20

More and more I run into people who are quite open about not believing in God. They are often quite strong in their beliefs, and as spiritual warriors, we Catholics also should be strong. As Scripture says, "He who is in you is greater than he who is in the world" (1 John 4:4). We also have the love of Christ, which allows us to speak the truth in love, rather than refute atheistic claims in any kind of antagonistic way.

Recently I had an e-mail exchange with an ex-Catholic who is now a self-proclaimed atheist (I'll call him "Richard"). He attended Catholic schools from kindergarten through twelfth grade. He graduated from Cal State Northridge with a degree in engineering. He now believes that there are no proven miracles, God is a myth, and the biblical narratives are fairy tales. Below are some samples of our correspondence.

When you die you die, that's it. Deal with it—there is no afterlife. Religion is a crutch for weak people that don't think rationally. Nobody knows what happens when you die; religious people engage in pure speculation.

Everybody in the world is going to die; we can agree that the death ratio is still hovering around 100 percent. Let's imagine, though, that you are trapped in a cage with a hungry lion. You suddenly notice a door in the corner that may offer a way of escape. Wouldn't you try to run to that door and get to the other side? Granted, you don't *know* what's on the other side of that door. But you do know what's in the cage: certain death by the jaws and claws of a lion.

Many atheists are like the person described above. Jesus said, "I am the door" (John 10:7). Can you trust him? I do, because he has demonstrated that he can be trusted. The atheist position of "staying in the cage" actually becomes a foolish, reckless attempt to gamble with one's soul. Running for that door—even though you are not sure what is on the other side, or if anything is on the other side—has to be better than staying in the cage with a hungry lion. To stay in the cage with the lion is sure death, while to go through the door may lead to safety, which is a bet any sane person would want to take.

I have read enough to be convinced beyond a reasonable doubt that there is no afterlife. I truly believe that we're all headed to the grave and then total extinction of the soul.

Blaise Pascal argues that we have two basic choices—and either way we must take the risk of being wrong. If we put our faith in God and it turns out that God does not exist after all, we face a small downside risk: We die and simply evaporate; we cease to exist, with no memory, no imagination, no understanding (so we wouldn't even know we had been wrong). However, if we reject God during the course of our lives, and then die only to find out that he does exist, we face a much more serious risk: eternal separation from God in hell.

Based on these two possible outcomes, Pascal argues that it is much riskier to be an atheist. In the face of an uncertain outcome, no rational person would refuse to give up something that is finite if there is the possibility of gaining an infinite prize. In fact, under these conditions, it is irrational not to believe. Pascal wrote, "Let us weigh up the gain and loss involved in calling heads that God exists. If you win, you win everything. If you lose, you lose nothing. Do not hesitate, then: Wager that he exists."[5]

The ingenuity of Pascal's argument is that it emphasizes the practical necessity of making a choice. This necessity is imposed by death. There comes a day when there will be no more tomorrow."[6] Personally, I would rather live my life as if there is a God and die to find out there isn't than live my life as if there isn't and die to find out there is.

If there is a God, why does he hide himself from us? This feels like a big hide-and-seek game, and it doesn't make sense to me. Why doesn't God just prove himself to us?

Many people wonder why God does not make his presence more obvious. The popular American astronomer Carl Sagan once suggested that in order to dispel all doubts about his existence, "God could have engraved the ten commandments on the moon." Pascal supplied a plausible reason for what he called "the hiddenness of God." He wrote, "Perhaps God wants to hide himself from those who have no desire to encounter him, while revealing himself to those whose hearts are open. If God were to declare himself beyond our ability to reject him, then we would be forced to believe." Pascal is saying that perhaps God wants to be known only by the creatures who seek him.[7]

The existence of a God makes no sense to me, but atheism makes complete common sense and scientific sense to me.

My definition of atheism is the belief that there was nothing, and nothing happened to nothing, and then nothing magically exploded for no reason, creating everything, and then a bunch of nothing magically rearranged itself for no reason whatsoever into a self-replicating something, which then turned into dinosaurs. *Makes perfect sense to me.*

For me, life without God is like an unsharpened pencil; it has no point.

Evolution is a scientific fact. You need to go back to school and hit the science books—your religion has blinded you from the hard facts.

The simple truth is that no evidence for macroevolution exists. I repeat the words of well-known journalist and philosopher Malcolm Muggeridge: "I am convinced that the theory of evolution…will be one of the great jokes in the history books of the future. Posterity will marvel that so very flimsy and dubious a hypothesis could be accepted with the incredible credulity that it has."[8]

By the way, it was a Catholic priest, Fr. George Lemaitre (1894-1966), who proposed that the universe was not eternal but began when a primordial atom exploded billions of years ago. Lemaitre was the pioneer of the big-bang theory. God was the cause of the big bang, which caused everything to exist out of nothing.

"For the scientist who has lived by his faith in the power of reason, the story ends like a bad dream. He has scaled the mountain of ignorance, he is able to conquer the highest peak; as he pulls himself over the final rock, he is greeted by a band of theologians who have been sitting there for centuries."[9]

Anybody who believes in God is foolish. All you have to do is go to college and study science so that you can see the error of your faith-based ways. I take pride in my studies, and I choose to bow before the altar of science and reason.

At its root, atheism is a moral problem. It is not that atheists *can't* believe in the existence of God, it's that they don't *want* to believe in the existence of God. Why? Because this would cause them to be bound by moral absolutes. Humility is required to seek and to encounter the face of God. Bishop Fulton Sheen said, "Humility is always the condition of discovering divinity."

"The fool says in his heart, 'There is no God'" (Psalm 14:1). Atheism is a problem of the heart, not the head. Frankly, I don't have enough faith to be an atheist.

Richard, do you really think we are just a collection of cells and molecules that coincidentally came together? Are we just a bunch of atoms ruled by deterministic scientific law? Are we just a quivering mass of unfulfilled protoplasm? To me, it takes more faith to believe this than it takes to believe in a supernatural being called God who created us. Darwinian evolution is unproved; there are no fossil records to support evolution. Random chance renders evolution improbable and impossible, and empirical science militates against the theory of evolution.

Science and religion are not compatible. Catholicism is anti-science.

I don't see any conflict between science and religion, for all truth comes from God. Scientific truth and religious truth come from the same source: God. Many scientists, however, have an anti-supernatural bias—believing that only what can be seen is real.

> Though faith is above reason, there can never be any real discrepancy between faith and reason. Since the same God who reveals mysteries and infuses faith has bestowed the light of reason on the human mind, God cannot deny himself, nor can truth ever contradict truth. Consequently, methodical research in all branches of knowledge, provided it is carried out in a truly scientific manner and does not override moral laws, can never conflict with the faith, because the things of the world and the things of faith derive from the same God.

The humble and persevering investigator of the secrets of nature is being led, as it were, by the hand of God in spite of himself, for it is God, the conserver of all things, who made them what they are. (*CCC* 159)

You have given me some food for thought, I will admit. I have never witnessed a man of faith explain his faith in God by using science, and I commend you. But what about all the evil done by religion? That alone is a compelling argument that keeps me away from religion.

You talk about all the evil done by religion. I will grant you that there is good religion and bad religion. Sometimes good people do bad things in the name of religion. Looking at history, however, it's clear that totalitarian regimes governed by atheist leaders have caused far more bloodshed than Christians. For instance, Stalin was responsible for around 20 million deaths during World War I. Mao Tse Tung's Communist China regime killed about 70 million people. Adolph Hitler comes in a distant third, with about 10 million murders (6 million of which were Jews) in Nazi Germany. Cambodian leader Pol Pot killed about 2 million of his fellow countrymen. Dictators such as Lenin, Castro, Khrushchev and many others also have been responsible for mass killings.[10]

Religiously inspired casualties simply cannot compete with the murders perpetrated by atheist regimes. The Crusades, the Inquisition, and the Salem witch burnings account for a small percentage of the deaths as compared to nonbelievers.

Sixty years ago, in a remarkable book called *The Drama of Atheist Humanism*, Fr. Henri de Lubac exposed this false humanism as well as its lethal consequences for Western civilization. The deliberate rejection of God cannot be the road to authentic human liberation. Indeed, the contrary is the case. Contemplating the tragic history of the twentieth century, Pope John Paul II saw with utter clarity that the eclipse of God leads not to greater human *liberation* but to the most dire human *peril*. Man without God is not freer. He is in greater danger. This is what Pope John Paul II meant by the phrase "culture of death." In the words of Fr. Lubac: "It is not true, as is sometimes said, that man cannot organize the world without God. What is true is that, without God, he can only organize it against man."[11]

For Reflection

1. How comfortable do you feel conversing with someone who doesn't believe in God?

2. On a scale of one to ten, how would you rate your confidence level when it comes to sharing your faith?

3. If you answered with a number seven or below, what makes you feel uncomfortable? What might you do to increase your confidence level?

CHAPTER FOUR

No Chance Encounters

God did not give us a spirit of timidity but a spirit of power
and love and self-control.
—2 Timothy 1:7

I was invited to speak at the South Texas Men's Conference in 1999. Sponsored by the Archdiocese of San Antonio, Texas, it was held right before the Jubilee Year 2000, and excitement and anticipation could be felt in the convention center where five thousand men were gathered. There was an impressive list of speakers at this conference: Scott Hahn, Marcus Grodi, Jeff Cavins, Curtis Martin—men of God and men of valor who have touched my life in profound ways with their teachings and love for Scripture. I was honored to be on the same platform.

The conference finished at about 5:00 p.m. Saturday, and I left for the airport and boarded the plane for the three-hour flight back to California. I began thinking about getting home, tackling my boys, hugging my daughter, and spending a quiet evening at home in my wife's arms. Since there were about eighty-five empty seats and only fifteen passengers, the flight attendant told us that we could sit anywhere we wanted. I made a beeline for the very back of the plane, where I had four seats to myself with no one around me for ten rows. I was tired from the conference, so I planned to stretch out across those four seats as soon as the captain said we could unbuckle our seatbelts. I took out a copy of *This Rock* magazine, looking forward to catching up on some spiritual reading.

As I began reading I sensed danger and the presence of evil. I think it was a combination of my police training and the gift of discernment. As I looked up, I saw a woman walking down the aisle toward me. She was really exaggerating her walk, moving her hips from left to right as if she was walking down the ramp of a beauty pageant. I noticed that she was dressed very immodestly. As she walked her long hair bounced from left to right, and she ran her fingers through it several times. She was pretty and she knew it.

She had the attention of every male on the plane, from the stewards to the passengers. I said to myself, *OK, time to take custody of the eyes,* and I looked down and began reading my magazine again. Well, lo and behold, this woman walked all the way to the back of the plane (passing almost eighty empty seats) and sat right next to me. The flight attendant told us to fasten our seatbelts, and we took off.

My police training made me think this lady was a prostitute. I didn't want to make it obvious that I didn't want to sit next to her, but I decided that when we were able to unbuckle our seatbelts and walk around, I would simply find another seat on the plane. For many men (Catholic or not), sitting next to a young, scantily clad prostitute whose perfume could be detected ten rows away could be a near occasion of sin, unwise and imprudent. It was especially true for someone happily married like me. I looked out the window and read my magazine.

She kept trying to talk to me as she applied fire-red lipstick and brushed her long hair. I exchanged pleasantries with her, telling her that I had been in San Antonio on business and was headed back home. She replied that she was on business, too, and then made some sexual innuendos. I was caught off guard at how bold and brazen she was.

At first I felt intimidated because I had dealt with women like this during my law enforcement days. Often they were cold, calculating, calloused women who would steal anything that wasn't nailed down. I also knew that they were wounded sinners; so many men had lied to them, beat them, humiliated them, cursed at them, stolen from them, and used them that they developed hardened hearts. This is the consequence of a life of sin, and I knew how strong the pull of lust, promiscuity, and fornication can be and how it can enslave a person.

Jesus answered them, "Truly, truly, I say to you, every one who commits sin is a slave to sin." (John 8:34)

Do you not know that if you yield yourselves to any one as obedient slaves, you are slaves of the one whom you obey, either of sin, which leads to death, or of obedience, which leads to righteousness? (Romans 6:16)

She began speaking very seductively to me. Here she was, invading my space and privacy, so I tried to intimidate her by telling her that I was a Los Angeles deputy sheriff. Undeterred, she immediately said very sensuously that she gave special discounts to law enforcement officers!

At this point I heard the words of Jesus in my mind: "You will know the truth, and the truth will make you free" (John 8:32). For some reason I sensed that this woman was a fallen-away Catholic. I reached into my suitcase and took out my sword (the Holy Bible). She leaned over and tried to whisper in my ear the different things that she was offering and her price. I said to myself in a soft whisper, "Speak to me, Lord; your servant is listening." I opened my Bible, and it fell open to 2 Timothy 1:6–8. I read,

For this reason I remind you to rekindle the gift of God that is within you through the laying on of my hands; for God did not give us a spirit of timidity but a spirit of power and love and self-control.

Do not be ashamed then of testifying to our Lord….

I flipped to another page and read, "Do not be afraid, but speak and do not be silent; for I am with you" (Acts 18:9–10). I turned to one last page, and my eyes fell upon, "Little children, you are of God, and have overcome them; for he who is in you is greater than he who is in the world" (1 John 4:4).

I felt like Popeye who had just opened a can of spinach! I was now ready to speak like a lion breathing fire. I turned to her quickly and, with a surge of inspiration, I said, "Shame on you! Don't you know that you are already married to someone? I know that you are a fallen-away Catholic, and you belong to *Jesus*. You are his bride—you are consecrated to him!"

She look at me, stunned, and admitted that she was a Catholic who had not been inside a Catholic Church since she made her first Holy Communion at the age of seven. She also shared that she had been a prostitute since she was eighteen. She was now twenty-eight, living in Las Vegas, where she plied her trade. I suspected that she was also a drug addict who sold her body to support her habit. I had two options:

I could get up, move to a different seat, and go back to reading my magazine, telling myself, *Tough luck—she's all screwed up; she doesn't know Jesus. She's on her way to hell.*

I could listen to Jesus's words: "Go into all the world and preach the gospel to the whole creation…in my name they will cast out demons" (Mark 16:15, 17). As the *Catechism* says, "…the true apostle is on the

lookout for occasions of announcing Christ by word, either to unbe-
lievers or the lay faithful" (*CCC* 905).

I knew this was not a chance encounter but had been ordained by
God. "Divine providence works also through the actions of creatures.
To human beings God grants the ability to cooperate freely with his
plans" (*CCC* 323*).* I began to tell her about salvation history and how
God has provided his Son Jesus Christ to save, sanctify, and set her
free. Her countenance began to change from one of sexual aggres-
sion to humility, and suddenly I could tell that the gospel was making
sense to her. *I knew that her heart longed for God* (see Psalm 42:1). As
I spoke to her about the Lord Jesus, she covered her chest with her
arms. I took off my jacket and lent it to her so she would not feel
embarrassed. She said, "That's funny, I've never been embarrassed to
expose myself before any man, but I feel embarrassed in front of you."

Since we had a three-hour flight ahead of us, I began sharing the
beauty of our Catholic faith with this lost soul. I told her that many
people will miss heaven by twelve inches—the distance from their
head to their heart. I showed her John 3:16—"For God [the greatest
lover] so loved the world [the greatest amount of people] that he
gave his only-begotten Son [the greatest gift], that whoever believes
in him should not perish [the greatest hope] but have eternal life [the
greatest reward]"—and I told her how this is the greatest love story
ever told because it involves each of us and God.

She began to weep. Three hours on an airplane began to heal so
many years of having a broken heart as a result of sin. She asked me if
God could ever forgive her for the last ten years of her life as a prostitute and all that came with it. I shared the following verses with her:

> Though your sins are like scarlet,
>> they shall be as white as snow. (Isaiah 1:18)

The Lord is merciful and gracious,
> slow to anger and abounding in mercy. (Psalm 103:8)

I, I am He
> who blots out your transgressions for my own sake,
> and I will not remember your sins. (Isaiah 43:25)

As she cried tears of pain, healing, and joy, I told her that God's mercy is greater than his justice. I shared Joel 2:25 with her: "I will restore to you the years which the swarming locust has eaten."

As the plane began its descent into Burbank, she said to me, "Every time you show me something from the Bible, *my heart starts burning—I know it's true.*" She used the same words that disciples on the road to Emmaus said about the risen Lord Jesus Christ after he vanished from their sight—"were not our hearts burning within us?" (see Luke 24:32).

When we landed, we walked together toward the baggage claim area. I let her keep my jacket so that she would not bring undue attention to herself. I had a Catholic prayer book and a booklet called "Let There Be Light" in my carry-on, and I gave these to her as we were waiting for our luggage. She said tearfully, "I want to have Jesus in my heart." I said, "Let's pray," and she said, "Where?" I said, "Right here!"

She closed her eyes, and I led her into a heartfelt prayer of repentance and willingness to open her heart to Jesus and to proclaim him as her Lord and Savior. Weeping, she repeated every single word I said. I told her to go to a Catholic Church as soon as possible and make an appointment with a priest and go to confession.

Her parting words to me were, "I had bad intentions when I saw you in the back of that plane. I thought you were some wealthy businessman. I have been intimate with over a thousand men in the last ten years. Men have lied to me, raped me, abused me, hit me, stolen from me, cursed at me, disrespected me, etc. You are the first man in my life to talk to me about Jesus."

I responded, "Whatever good I do comes from God, and I thank him for it." We said good-bye and I wished her God's blessing. I hope she follows through with her newfound commitment, because then I will see her again—this time in her white baptismal garments, when Jesus comes back at the resurrection of the elect.

As people of faith, we have an advantage in life. We wake up with a purpose. We have a sense of mission, and this gives our lives enduring meaning. Those like this prostitute are "wandering generalities" that serve the unholy trinity of "me, myself, and I" as a result of their sinful lifestyles. But we serve a God of resurrection. We can share with confidence the Word of God, no matter what circumstances we find ourselves in. There are no chance encounters!

For Reflection

1. Have you ever found yourself seated next to someone who wanted to engage you in conversation? What response have you had? Has the Holy Spirit been able to use you in an unexpected way? If so, how?

2. When you see someone who fits a particular stereotype, how adept are you at looking beyond appearances to the real person beneath the façade?

3. How comfortable are you praying with someone in public? What steps could you take to be more confident about this?

CHAPTER FIVE

Warriors Come in All Sizes

O Jesus, if one day with your help I can do any good, here I
am in the ranks of your fighting men.[12]
—Pope John XXIII

The story of David and Goliath is one of my favorites. Have you
ever been made fun of by a big bully? I have. It doesn't feel good to
be taunted. Goliath was a huge man. He was a giant that might have
stood between nine and eleven feet tall. This Philistine cursed at the
Israelites and said disparaging things about their God. He wanted to
settle the battle with the Israelites in a one-on-one contest to avoid
having so many soldiers die. He asked to fight just one Israelite, but
everyone was terrified of him.

At the time, David was just an ordinary kid. He was not exactly the
next "Achilles" or "King Leonidas" in the eyes of his older brothers or
anyone else for that matter.

The Israelites were ruled by King Saul. His days were spent orga-
nizing Israel's militia to oppose the Philistines, who were expanding
into traditional Israelite territory. His were days of hard fighting and
a life spent in a rough-hewn fortress. Unlike other kings, Saul had no
palace, or any of the trappings typical that went with it. Yet King Saul
continued to defeat the numerous enemies surrounding his infant
nation.

The setting for this story is one of King Saul's many confrontations
with the Philistines, this time the two armies are facing each other
across the valley of Elah, some fifteen miles west of Bethlehem. The

Philistines secret weapon was the giant Goliath of Gath, who was so formidable in his armor that not even King Saul, who was the tallest of the Israelites would face him in a fight. Every day for forty days, Goliath challenged any Israelite to single combat, with the Israelite's freedom or slavery resting on the outcome.

Bringing food to his three eldest brothers in the army, young David saw the giant. Goliath's defiance infuriated David, who was absolutely confident that God could give the victory over any Philistine. David volunteered to fight Goliath, telling the king how he had "killed both lions and bears" (1 Samuel 17:36) with his bare hands. Against all expectations and with the fate of his whole kingdom at stake, King Saul allowed this youth to fight Goliath. David rejected the offer to put on King Saul's battle armor and instead took only his familiar slingshot. While this seems almost foolhardy to us today, the slingshot was a common and powerful weapon used in ancient warfare. Excellent "slingers" could propel heavy, three-inch stones up to 150 miles per hour with deadly accuracy.

The arrogant Goliath was insulted to have his challenge to fight answered by a young boy. But David returned the giant's disdain with a promise to cut off Goliath's head to show that "the Lord saves not with sword and spear; for the battle is the Lord's" (1 Samuel 17:47). Little David ran straight at Goliath and, with a single throw, killed the giant with a stone that hit him in the forehead. David then unsheathed the fallen giant's sword and beheaded him, as the exultant Israelites charged across the valley to destroy the Philistine army. David carried Goliath's head and presented it to King Saul. After listening to Goliath antagonize the Israelites for forty days, David was angered by such an arrogant pagan insulting the living God. David was transformed from a mere youth to a courageous warrior.

We could call this David's personal desert experience. From this day forward, David became popular with the Israelite masses.

David has clearly been the runt of the family his whole life; this makes his courage even more impressive. It would be one thing if the eldest of a noble family thought he had what it took to square off with Goliath. But the youngest of eight brothers, who up until now has been in charge of watching the sheep while the "real men" wage war against Israel's enemies? David didn't let Goliath's size or his weapons intimidate him—his focus was on God and his strength and power. Although David was just a young brave boy, he knew that God protected him from the bears and lions that tried to steal the sheep he was guarding and had given him the courage to kill a lion and a bear with his bare hands.

Although Goliath had a suit of armor, all David had was a slingshot and five smooth stones. Saul wanted David to wear the king's own armor to protect him, but it was very heavy and David had never fought while wearing it. So he left it behind and instead trusted God: "The Lord…will deliver me from the hand of this Philistine" (1 Samuel 17:37). Saul then tells David what every Catholic hears at the end of Mass: "Go, and the Lord be with you!" (v.38). After we receive God's grace (strength) through his Word and through the Holy Eucharist, we too are sent into the world to wage spiritual warfare.

David's success in overcoming Goliath began his career as a warrior. He eventually became known as the best warrior in all of ancient history, with the Bible saying that David had slain "his ten thousands" (1 Samuel 18:7).

David grabbed five stones, even though he kills Goliath with the first one. Some ancient sources say that the five stones could stand for the Torah (the first five books of the Bible). I've also heard that the five stones can also stand for the five decades of the rosary. Maybe they represented the five senses of Goliath that were hardened against God. And there are five stones we have access to today to fight against the Goliaths in our world:

1. Prayer
2. Holy Eucharist
3. Holy Bible
4. Fasting
5. Confession

We all have fears; we all encounter enemies. But we don't have to be afraid. Jesus is always with us to protect us and give us courage. We only have to remember that *the battle is the Lord's*. When Jesus gives us the victory, let's be sure to thank him and praise him for what he has done.

OUR MARCHING ORDERS

"The sons of Israel went up out of the land of Egypt equipped for battle." (Exodus 13:18)

"And that all this assembly may know that the Lord saves not with sword and spear; for the battle is the Lord's." (1 Samuel 17:47)

"Thus says the Lord to you, 'Fear not, and be not dismayed at this great multitude; for the battle is not yours but God's.'" (2 Chronicles 20:15)

"'You will not need to fight in this battle; take your position, stand still, and see the victory of the Lord on your behalf, O Judah and Jerusalem.' Fear not, and be not dismayed; tomorrow go out against them, and the Lord will be with you." (2 Chronicles 20:17)

"For you girded me with strength for the battle; you made my assailants sink under me." (Psalm 18:39)

"Who is the King of glory? The Lord, strong and mighty, the Lord, mighty in battle!" (Psalm 24:8)

"O Lord, my Lord, my strong deliverer, you have covered my head in the day of battle." (Psalm 140:7)

"Blessed be the Lord, my rock, who trains my hands for war, and my fingers for battle." (Psalm 144:1)

"Then the Lord will go forth and fight against those nations as when he fights on a day of battle." (Zechariah 14:3)

"For everything there is a season…a time for war, and a time for peace." (Ecclesiastes 3:1, 8)

"No weapon that is fashioned against you shall prosper, and you shall confute every tongue that rises against you in judgment. This is the heritage of the servants of the Lord and their vindication from me, says the Lord." (Isaiah 54:17)

For Reflection

1. Are there any "Goliaths" in your life? What do they look like?
2. What is your plan to defeat the Goliaths in your life?
3. What does the verse mean: "The battle is not yours but God's"? Have there been times when you tried to fight in your own strength against an obstacle or situation? What has been the result?

CHAPTER SIX

Raising Daughters for Christ

Charm is deceitful, and beauty is vain,
but a woman who fears the LORD is to be praised.
—Proverbs 31:30

My daughter, Annmarie, has been gifted with good looks, intelligence, and athletic ability. She is also a young person of deep faith. She has always been very open to attending Mass on Sundays, daily prayer, the devotions of the Church, talking with me about growing in her faith and the importance of chastity, and going on retreats and conferences. She attended a Catholic high school here in southern California.

When Annmarie was in the ninth grade, she told me that all her friends were dating. She asked, "Daddy, when can *I* start dating?" I explained to her that dating in high school was nothing but a distraction, and that she was too young and immature to be dating. I told her to concentrate on her studies, her sports, and her faith. Dating could wait until she graduated from high school and started college. Her first reaction was, "But Dad, *everybody* else is allowed to date starting in ninth grade." I reminded her that I was not *everybody's* dad—I was *her* dad, and any rules were for her spiritual, physical, and emotional benefit.

One reason so many young people make mistakes where chastity is concerned is that "Research has shown that the prefrontal cortex— the home of good judgment, common sense, impulse control and emotions—is not completely mature until children are 20-22 years of age," according to Dr. Sharon Cooper, a pediatrician at the University of North Carolina.[13]

I told my daughter that I love her more than any other man out there. I also told her that when I did allow her to date, there would be ground rules. These are some of the principles of Christian dating:

Ask God's blessing at the beginning of a relationship and build that relationship upon Christ and his love.

Enter it with the purpose of discerning marriage; involve each other's families; be accountable to each other; and pace yourselves as you spend time together.

Always listen for the Lord's guidance.

My daughter was not very happy, but she was obedient. Numerous young people that went to high school with my daughter told me she honored my instruction and she didn't date.

I wanted my daughter to understand that there is nothing wrong with having friends and spending time with members of the opposite sex; however, committed relationships should be entered into with the consideration of discerning marriage. When we enter into dating relationships, we should allow wisdom to chaperone romance. I encouraged Annmarie to find another female that she looked up to, and go to her for guidance in her relationships—but this involves having the humility to become accountable to others. As the Bible says, "Without counsel plans go wrong, but with many advisers they succeed" (Proverbs 15:22).

My daughter began being asked out on dates in the ninth grade. She received invitations to all the school dances, and I kept saying no. She got so tired of asking me if she could date that she stopped bringing it up. One day, out of the blue, she told me she had seen someone wearing a purity ring (purity rings are an outward symbol of the decision to practice sexual abstinence before marriage), and she thought that would be a cool thing to wear to show others that she had made a commitment to God to be chaste and pure.

Annmarie made this commitment at a retreat she attended, and she took it seriously. I had drilled into my daughter ever since she was small that her body was a temple of the Holy Spirit and that she was meant to honor and glorify God with her body (see 1 Corinthians 6:19–20). She understood this and knew it was right thing to do. The chastity pledge that she signed is posted right on the wall between her bedroom and my wife and my bedroom. It reads:

I WILL WAIT

I know that my virginity is a gift
I give one time to only one person.
I pledge to give my virginity on my wedding day
to the love of my life, my future spouse.
I am worth waiting for.
Annmarie Romero
5-14-07

Discipline Matters

Once upon a time, when she was six years old and as cute as it gets, she misbehaved. I've forgotten exactly what she did, but it was a Romero felony. Being the law-and-order type of guy that I am, I sent my little cutie to her room and told her to wait for me. I fully intended to spank her, although I had never spanked her before. She was always so obedient that I never needed to. However, I thought that what she did warranted a little swat in the behind. I was thinking of these two verses from the book of Proverbs:

He who spares the rod hates his son, but he who loves him is diligent to discipline him. (Proverbs 13:24)

Do not withhold discipline from a child; if you beat him with a rod, he will not die. If you beat him with the rod you will save his life from Sheol. (Proverbs 23:13–14)

As I was walking to Annmarie's bedroom, my wife gave me the look of a mother in intercessory prayer. I also noticed that my eight-year-old son, Paul, and my four-year-old son, Joshua, were kneeling in the front yard before a statue of the Sacred Heart of Jesus and the Immaculate Heart of Mary. I heard Paul say, "Jesus, tell my daddy not to spank my sister," and then they both said, "Hail Mary, full of grace, the Lord is with thee…" I was witnessing some serious prayer power here! This was the mystical body of Christ in full battle array. As I walked passed my wife, she said, "You don't have to spank her—just talk to her in a loud voice; she'll get the message."

As I walked into Annmarie's room, she looked at me with her big brown eyes and said, "Daddy, Daddy, can I tell you something?"

I said, "Yes, go ahead, tell me."

She replied, "Daddy, you know how you always tell me I am a temple of the Holy Spirit?" I nodded yes.

She said, "You're not going to spank the temple of the Holy Spirit, are you?"

I burst out laughing and said, "Come over here and give me a big hug." I picked her up in my arms, and I told her lovingly but firmly that what she did wrong. I explained what I expected from her next time. She said, "OK, Daddy, OK—I love you." And to this day, I have never spanked my daughter.

Pure in Spirit

When Annmarie was a junior in high school, one day I picked her up after tennis practice and told her I had a surprise for her. I took her to a Christian gift shop at the mall, and I brought her to the section where they had a display of purity rings, and I told her to pick one. Her eyes got as big as saucers, and she said, "I have always wanted one of these!" She picked one out, I paid for it, and I kept the box with me as we walked back to my truck.

Since it was only a week before Christmas, Annmarie said, "Dad, when can I have it? Do I have to wait for Christmas?" I didn't respond; I just drove a few miles to a local Catholic church with a perpetual Adoration Chapel. I parked my truck and told Annmarie to follow me. We walked into the Adoration Chapel, and I said, "Let's kneel in front of Jesus." We both knelt about five feet away from our Lord in the Blessed Sacrament. I took her hand and placed the purity ring on her finger, as we prayed the *Anima Christi* together:

> Soul of Christ, sanctify me. Body of Christ, save me. Blood of Christ, inebriate me.
> Water from the side of Christ, wash me.
> Passion of Christ, strengthen me.
> Oh Good Jesus, hear me. Within your wounds, hide me.
> Separated from you let me never be. From the evil one, protect me.
> At the hour of my death, call me. And close to you bid me, That with your saints and angels I may praise you forever and ever. Amen.[14]

We also prayed the following prayer of St. Ignatius:

> Take Lord and receive all my liberty,
> my memory, my understanding, and my entire will.

All that I have and possess you have given all to me.

To you, oh Lord, I return it.

All is yours, dispose of it according to your holy will.

Give me your love and your grace for this is sufficient for me.[15]

Finally, we prayed a prayer of Marian consecration:

My Queen my Mother I give myself entirely to you;

and to show my devotion to you,

I consecrate to you this day, my eyes, my ears, my mouth, my heart,

my whole being without reserve.

Wherefore, most loving Mother, as I am your own, keep me, defend me as your property and possession Amen.[16]

My daughter got emotional, and so did I. We walked out in silence, both knowing how important this event was. We hugged each other as we walked back to my truck.

It was the Holy Spirit that inspired me to give my daughter a purity ring and put it on her finger in front of the Blessed Sacrament. I can only imagine that the heavens were rejoicing at the fact that a father was trying to prepare his daughter for the many assaults she would have to undergo as she would fight for her purity every day in this culture of death. I told my daughter that my prayer was for her future husband to take off that purity ring at the altar and replace it with her wedding ring.

As Christians, the family is a little Church. The fathers of the Church referred to the family as the "domestic Church," where the father represents Christ the priest, the mother is the spotless bride of Christ, and the children represent the faithful. The aim of any church should be the salvation and sanctification of all its members. The family should be a domestic Church whose goal is the salvation of its members.

A sacramental marriage provides the mutual assistance to help each other get to know and love God in this life and to be happy with him in the next. This relationship, however, is neither fluid nor manmade. Christ established the marital relationship for growing in holiness and obtaining salvation. Marriage and family life are meant to be a vocation to holiness—it's not a vocation to an easy life. Far from it! Marriage in the Catholic Church is extremely difficult, especially in light of the fact that our culture offers opposition to this view of marriage.

Advice for Young Women

I recommend that all young women make a short list of the qualities that they envision their future spouse having, as well as a short list of qualities he must not have. This helps a young women to think clearly when and if she finds someone and begins to have feelings for him. For example, a sample list might look something like the following.

My future husband must:

Be Catholic

Be invested in our children receiving a Catholic education

Earn a certain income so I can stay home and raise our children.

These lists require thought and prayer. Holy families don't just happen. Remember that the bait you use determines the kind of fish you catch. A noble man is attracted to an elegant and modestly dressed woman. On the other hand, if a woman wants to attract a man who is led by his feelings and acts upon impulse, a man who is here today and gone tomorrow, she will "fish" for him by dressing and acting immodestly.

The Beginning of the Relationship

The beginning of the spousal relationship is very important. The true purpose of dating is to determine whether marriage is in a couple's future. Recreational dating is really not appropriate for Catholics; dating is meant to be ordered toward a vocation. You don't expect a seminarian to be dating while he's in seminary, do you? It just stands to reason that if a young man is not ready to give up women, he is not ready to become a priest.

Young men must be mature enough to get married. He should be able to put a roof over her head and food on the table *before* he begins to date a girl. Young women need to be mature enough to assume the responsibilities of motherhood before they start dating.

One of the best places for a young woman to meet her future spouse is Sunday Mass. Other likely places include a Bible study or a conference attended by fervent Catholics, or at another Catholic couple's wedding.

When a young woman has the perspective that Christian marriage is a call from God, an invitation to assist her spouse to spend eternity with God, her whole perspective on dating will change. This is the wisdom I've tried to impart to Annmarie, even though it goes against the norms of our culture.

For Reflection

1. If you are a woman reading this book, how has your upbringing differed from the way Annmarie is being raised?
2. If you are a father of a daughter, how will the principles in this chapter affect the way you will parent your daughter? Are there any areas that need adjusting?
3. If you are single, what difference will the advice in this chapter make in your life and the way you view dating?

CHAPTER SEVEN

Raising Sons for Christ

Fathers, do not provoke your children to anger, but bring
them up in the discipline and instruction of the Lord.
—Ephesians 6:4

I have two young adult sons: Paul and Joshua. They are both aggressive wrestlers and jiu-jitsu competitors, yet they are good Catholics. They love the Lord and love the Church. I have tried to instill in my boys a sense of mission and purpose, and the following story speaks to their masculine heart and the warrior within them.

Vietnam veteran David Grossman says there are basically three types of people in our society: sheep, wolves, or sheepdogs. Most of the people in our society are sheep—"kind, gentle, decent peace-loving creatures who only hurt one another by accident."[17] Wolves, on the other hand, attack and prey on the sheep. They are vicious and are capable of evil deeds. The sheep often live in denial, not wanting to believe that such evildoers exist.

Finally, there are sheepdogs. Sheepdogs love the peace, just like the sheep. However, sheepdogs are committed to protecting the flock and confronting the wolves. A sheepdog has a warrior's heart; this is someone who is walking the hero's path, unafraid to enter the heart of darkness and come out unscathed.

Interestingly enough, the sheep generally do not like the sheepdog. He looks like a wolf. He has fangs and the capacity for violence. The sheepdog, unlike the wolf, would never do any harm to the sheep. Still, the sheepdog disturbs the sheep. He is a constant reminder that there are wolves in the land.

Let me add one last important component to the great insight given to us by Lt. Col. Grossman. There are three types of men to be sure, but there is also Jesus Christ, the God Man, who is in a league all by himself. Jesus is the Good Shepherd (see John 10:11). Jesus is our protector but he uses sheepdogs as the instruments of his protection.

God calls men to be leaders, protectors, and providers. A man's task and mission is to evangelize his family, lead them by example, and help them get to heaven. Jesus is the perfect example of what every man should strive to emulate. Jesus Christ our role model is the Lamb of God (John 1:29) and the lion of Judah (Revelation 5:5). Jesus Christ is the perfect lover and perfect fighter.

Every woman wants her man to be a lamb in terms of his sacrificial love, and she wants a lion to lead and protect her amd guide her to a life of holiness.

I've made sure my sons know the importance of being sexually pure. I even created a talk just for them—complete with a PowerPoint slide presentation—that I often share with them on Sunday evenings. My sons (and daughter) have gone with me to pray in front of the local abortion clinic with my wife and me many times—they've even observed their peers going into the clinic. I tell them that making the choice to stay pure isn't easy, but by hindsight they will be so glad they did. To make sure they understand why they should wait to marry before they have sex, I've shared with them the following list:

Why Wait? Ten Ways

1. *Set limits.* You're worth waiting for!
2. *Put friendship first.* The woman you marry should be your best friend.
3. *Make sure those you date share your values.* Such a person will respect you and your standards.

4. *Choose supportive friends.* You can help each other stay strong.

5. *Be prepared for temptation.* Don't be surprised when you find yourself tempted, and have faith that you can overcome it.

6. *Say no to drugs and alcohol.* These substances weaken your willpower.

7. *Understand the consequences of being sexually active.* Pregnancy, sexually transmitted diseases, emotional issues…. Know the painful price of impurity.

8. *Trust your parents and their wisdom.* Never be afraid to discuss concerns and questions with them.

9. *Plan creative dates.* Group activities, daytime outings—enjoy getting to know each other in safe, wholesome situations.

10. *Don't focus on physical intimacy.* Let your relationship grow in other healthy ways first.[18]

Brave Hearts

Catholic men must have brave hearts. This is the opposite of being a coward, which is "one who shows disgraceful fear or timidity," according to the dictionary.[19] A coward lacks the courage to do or endure dangerous or unpleasant things.

Too many men sink to the level of being a coward these days. Most men don't want to be considered cowards, although sadly some men are just fine with the label. But God did not create men to be cowards.

A lot of guys see themselves as being brave because they sound brave. They talk a big game around their friends, or maybe they stand out for doing something amazing in the area of sports. They could even take a risk in the business world and look really courageous. But in God's economy, this doesn't cut it. The true test of courage is when a man is confronted with standing up for those things that are truly noble and sacred.

When a man turns his back on defending a woman or just uses a woman, doesn't defend children or stand up for the unborn, doesn't defend the sacredness of marriage or the teachings of the Catholic Church, then he has stepped into the coward zone. He should turn in his man card.

I have raised my boys to be sheepdogs in the service of Jesus Christ, the Good Shepherd. I've told them they are called to defend their mother, their sister, and stand up for any defenseless person. My prayer is that as they grow into adulthood they will develop the grace to be deeply courageous and full of zeal to "fight the good fight" of faith (see 1 Timothy 6:12). I am raising kingdom warriors who are battle-ready!

My oldest son, Paul, is in the army reserves. One day he showed me something called the "Soldier's Creed." I liked it so much that I decided to create a Catholic soldier's creed:

A Catholic Soldier's Creed (based on 2 Timothy 2:3–4)
I am a soldier of GOD. I am a warrior and a member of TEAM JESUS. I serve the "People of GOD" and live the Christian virtues and values. I shall always place the mission first. I shall never quit. Surrender is not an option. I shall never leave a fallen Catholic comrade. I am disciplined. I am physically, morally, mentally, and spiritually as tough as nails. I am trained and proficient in my spiritual warrior tasks and skills. I always maintain my spiritual weapons, my equipment, and myself. I am an expert and in the sure knowledge and practice of my Catholic faith. I stand ready to deploy, engage, and destroy the enemies of GOD in close and immortal combat. I am a guardian of the glorious freedom of the children of GOD and the Christian way of life. I am a soldier of GOD.[20]

For Reflection

1. When you were growing up, did anyone instill a sense of mission and purpose within you? If you answered yes, describe this.

2. If you are a parent of a son (or sons), how are you teaching them to be courageous men of valor, especially in the spiritual realm? What kingdom values are you instilling in them?

3. What examples of "brave hearts" do you see around you? What are some distinguishing marks?

CHAPTER EIGHT

How the Rosary Saved My Life

From the most ancient times the Blessed Virgin has been honored with the title of Mother of God, to whose protection the faithful fly in all their dangers and needs.

—CCC 971

It was March 3, 1991. I was asleep with my wife in the bedroom of our two-story home in Lake View Terrace, California. At the time I was a Los Angeles County deputy sheriff working the patrol division at the East L.A. Sheriff's Station. My two-year-old son, our first-born, was asleep in his bedroom. I was scheduled to be off for the next week. I was looking forward to a vacation with my beloved wife, Anita, and our baby, Paul.

I was awakened from a sound sleep by hearing police sirens—it sounded like they were right outside my bedroom window. One gets used to emergency vehicle sirens living in southern California; it's par for the course. However, something seemed different this time. I jumped out of bed and looked out the window, and I could see several LAPD patrol cars stopped on Foothill Boulevard and Osborne Street, about six blocks from our house. My own police instinct told me that they had just caught a wanted felon or a fleeing suspect. I felt safe seeing so many police cars in my neighborhood. I walked over to my son's bedroom to check on him. He was sound asleep; the sirens had not woken him. I laid my hand on his head and prayed, "May the Lord bless you, may the Lord keep you safe, may the Lord shine his face upon you all the days of your life, in Jesus name through Our

Lady's intercession, Amen." As the head of my household, I recite this prayer every night so the Lord would protect him and keep him safe in the secular violent culture that he would grow up in. In addition, I took holy water and blessed my wife and our bedroom, asking the Lord and Our Lady to place a hedge of protection over our house from the evil that lurks around us. I went back to bed with an incredible sense of peace.

The next morning, as I was eating breakfast with my family and beginning to enjoy the first day of my weeklong vacation, I turned on the television. The local news media broadcast the following:

> [On] March 3, 1991, Rodney King and two passengers were driving west on the Foothill Freeway and were apprehended by four members of the Los Angeles Police Department (LAPD) after a high speed pursuit. King was tackled, tasered, and heavily beaten with clubs by the officers. The incident, without the first few minutes during which police claim King was violently resisting arrest, was captured on camcorder by Argentine George Holliday from his apartment in the vicinity.[21]

The police officers claimed that King appeared to be under the influence of PCP,[22] a mind-altering drug that dulls the nervous system and makes one impervious to pain and also gives a person an incredible surge of strength. King had led police on a high-speed car chase and, after driving through several red lights and boulevard stops, had pulled over in the Lake View Terrace district. In a later interview, King, who was on parole from prison on a robbery conviction and who had past convictions for assault, battery, and robbery,[23] said that he led police on the high-speed car chase because he feared apprehension and being returned to prison for parole violations.

The footage of King being beaten by police officers while lying on the ground became an international media sensation and a rallying point for activists in Los Angeles and around the United States. Coverage was extensive during the initial two weeks after the incident: The *Los Angeles Times* published fifty-five articles, the *New York Times* published twenty-one articles, and the *Chicago Tribune* published fifteen articles. Eight stories appeared on *ABC News,* including a sixty-minute special on *Primetime Live.* The majority of the media coverage interpreted the incident as a shocking tragedy and accused the police of abusing their power.[24]

Before I finished my breakfast, the phone rang. It was my watch commander from the East L.A. Sheriff's station. He told me that all vacations had been cancelled and that I was to report to work as soon as possible in anticipation of riots throughout Los Angeles County as a result of the Rodney King arrest. I sensed that this was going to be a bad few days for the people of Los Angeles, especially the good and decent people who are the majority.

I prepared my gear for work and put on my uniform. I put on a light windbreaker to conceal my sheriff's uniform. My wife nervously told me to be careful, and she begged me to go straight to the freeway and to avoid the now-infamous intersection of Foothill Blvd and Osborne Street where King was arrested because there would probably be many media cameras, reporters, and anti-police activists there.

Well, I was just like a little child that is told, "Don't go into Mommy's bedroom because there are Christmas gifts that I have to wrap," who inevitably runs into the bedroom to investigate what was forbidden. Off I went to work in my Chevy El Camino, but instead of getting on the freeway, I drove south toward that intersection, curious to see if anything was happening there. On the way I prayed the Driver's Prayer to the Sacred Heart of Jesus. My mother had told me often that anyone who is devoted to the Sacred Heart of Jesus will find comfort in their afflictions and Our Lord will be their secure refuge in life and in death, and these promises gave me great consolation.

Driver's Prayer

Sacred Heart of Jesus, grant me
a steady hand and watchful eye,
that none be hurt as I pass by.
Thou givest life. I pray no act of mine
take away or mar that gift Divine.
Protect those, Lord, who travel with me
from highway dangers and all anxiety.
Teach me to use my car for others' needs
and never miss the beauty of Thy
world through excessive speed.
I pledge to drive with loving concern
to my every destination,
offering each travel hour to Thee
in a spirit of reparation.
Most Sacred Heart of Jesus,
my auto Companion,
have mercy on me.[25]

Into the Fray

From a distance I could make out a mob of people hanging around the intersection of the Rodney King arrest. Traffic was unusually slow. As I got closer, I could see at least a hundred young black men wielding bats, bricks, and rocks. I could see that they were stopping all the cars in front of me, blocking their access—much like a government checkpoint when crossing the border. As they got closer to me, I saw that they would look inside each car, and if the driver wasn't black, they would break all the windows of the car. Other individuals would jump on the hood and roof of the car. Once the car windows were broken, these criminals would punch the driver in the face with their closed fist as he or she sat immobile and helpless. Whether the car's occupants were young or old, if they weren't black, the thugs attacked them, shouting racial slurs.

Observing all this, I immediately thought, *Why didn't I listen to Anita?* I saw that there were about ten cars behind me, so there was no way I could put my car in reverse. There were a half-dozen cars in front of me; I was creeping forward as though I were in line at the car wash. As I watched the people in front of me getting beat up mercilessly, I realized the acute danger that I was in. There were no police in the area, and I was wearing my deputy sheriff's uniform underneath a thin windbreaker. If they physically forced me out of my car, they would discover that I was a deputy sheriff and I would be a dead man.

As I thought about my wife and son back home, I decided in my heart that I was *not* going to be a victim of a violent crime at the hands of a bunch of thugs. They reminded me of Our Lord's words in Mark 7:21–23: "For from within, out of the heart of man, come evil thoughts, fornication, theft, murder, adultery, coveting, wickedness, deceit, licentiousness, envy, slander, pride, foolishness. All these evil things come from within, and they defile a man." I also took comfort in Psalm 139, which essentially says that *God knows the number of our days*, and so I reminded myself that God was in control of my life and the number of my days, not some thugs. That brought me peace and consolation.

As I continued to edge forward slowly, adrenaline started rushing throughout my body. I began to hyperventilate just the way I did in the locker room right before a boxing or karate match to get myself in the proper frame of mind to defend myself. It was my way of "being in the zone." At the same time I realized that this massive human assault against totally innocent people was demonic, orchestrated by a host of evil spirits.

Beads for the Battle

I grabbed my rosary, clinging to the promise of Genesis 3:15 that Our Lady has power and authority to crush the head of the devil. The *Catechism* says that life is a battle (see *CCC* 409), and I knew I was about to enter the lion's den. The only thing I could do was to trust in the Lord. The Holy Spirit brought Psalm 55:18 to my mind: "He will deliver my soul in safety from the battle that I wage, for many are arrayed against me." I began storming heaven; I prayed my rosary with deep faith and with loud vocal prayers that came from my heart.

I remembered what St. Alphonsus de Liguori said: "In every danger of forfeiting divine grace, we should think of Mary, and invoke her name, together with that of Jesus; for these two names always go together."[26] I also remembered Our Lady's promise to those who pray the holy rosary: "Whoever shall recite the Rosary devoutly…shall never be conquered by misfortune….You shall obtain all you ask of me by the recitation of the rosary."[27] St Louis de Montfort said the rosary "gives us victory over our enemies."[28]

I felt as if I was clothed with the full armor of God—with both faith and reason. So with my left hand I prayed the rosary (faith), and with my right hand I took out my nine-millimeter semi-automatic handgun from my briefcase and held it level with my stomach, pointed straight at my windshield with the safety off. I reckoned that

I had sixteen rounds in my handgun, two magazines with fifteen rounds each, and a box of another hundred rounds. I imagined what was going to happen—this is known as *visual simulation*, a technique taught to policemen, soldiers, and athletes, where you see yourself winning over and over again. I was mentally and physically prepared to defend myself and shoot anybody who would attack me in my car with their potentially deadly weapons (a bat or a brick to the head is a deadly weapon without a doubt), just as it says in the *Catechism* (see 2263–2265).

I approached the assembly line, the thugs stood in front of my car and blocked me, and I kept on praying *my beads for the battle* audibly and with much intensity. For a Catholic, the rosary is like David's slingshot—it looks simple and harmless, but it is a powerful tool in the hands of a prayer warrior. I kept my handgun against my stomach, pointed towards the front window with the safety off. Several thugs circled my car; at least six of them raised their bats over their heads. I could already sense the windows being totally smashed and my face and body being slashed with a thousand pieces of glass. I pointed my gun at the thug who was right next to my driver's window, and I began to squeeze the trigger. Suddenly he shouted at the rest of them, "Hey brothers, let him pass! He's cool, man, he's cool, he awright"!

I heard the others say, "Awright now." They all moved aside and opened up a passage for my car, and I drove through, still praying my rosary and still holding my handgun. As I drove off, I looked behind me. I saw the wave of thugs close the passage with their bodies as they continued the merciless beatings. I breathed a sigh of relief because I was not looking forward to shooting some young black man whose mind and heart was corrupted by sin and evil, even though the Church allows us to defend ourselves.

As I drove to East Los Angeles, I put my gun away in my brief-case. I continued to pray the rosary in thankfulness to Our Lady for sparing me from my enemies. Our Lady showed herself to be a mother to me on this day. The rosary became a battering ram that allowed me to pass through the valley of the shadow of death, and I was spared from evil.

I've asked myself many times, "Why was I allowed to pass?" I am sure that they did not see my gun, and I doubt that I intimidated them. I believe that they may have seen Our Lady. The Canticle of Canticles says, "Who is she that cometh forth as the morning rising, fair as the moon, bright as the sun, terrible as an army set in (battle) array?" (6:10, Douay-Rheims translation). Both John Paul II and Benedict XVI have said that this is a reference to the Blessed Virgin Mary. She is a Warrior Queen Mother that fights for her children. And I am not ashamed to tell you that I am a mama's boy! Yes, the Blessed Virgin Mary is my mother and protectoress. She has a long history of protecting her children. As the Memorare says:

> Remember, O most gracious Virgin Mary, that never was it known that anyone who fled to thy protection, implored thy help, or sought thy intercession was left unaided. Inspired by this confidence, I fly unto thee, O Virgin of virgins, my mother; to thee do I come, before thee I stand, sinful and sorrowful. O Mother of the Word Incarnate, despise not my petitions, but in thy mercy hear and answer me. Amen.

How true and how real this prayer became for me on March 3, 1991! Because of this incident, I want a BMW more than ever—I want to **B**ring **M**ary to the **W**orld.

Unleash the Power of the Rosary in Your Life

Without a doubt, America is at the most crucial moment of her history. As Cardinal Karol Wojtyla (now Pope St. John Paul II) said: "We are now standing in the face of the greatest historical confrontation humanity has gone through. I do not think that wide circles of the American society or wide circles of the Christian community realize this fully. We are now facing the final confrontation between the Church and the anti-Church, of the Gospel versus the anti-Gospel."[29]

All Catholics would do well to keep in mind the power of the rosary and the message of Fatima. The rosary is not merely a devotional aid; it is a weapon of conversion, protection, and love. The rosary was given to us for such a time as this—never has this weapon been more needed than it is today. Don't ever forget that you are a "soldier of Christ" (see 2 Timothy 2:3–5).

With the rosary in one hand, the Bible in your other, and Jesus and Mary in your heart, you are ready for action. Remember, "in all these things we are more than conquerors through him who loved us" (Romans 8:37), and "the people who know their God shall stand firm and take action" (Daniel 11:32). The following is something you might want to memorize as a reminder of the power and purpose of the rosary.

ROSARY CREED

I will pray the rosary diligently. I will pray harder than my enemy, Satan, who is trying to destroy me. I know that what counts in this war with Satan is not the number of prayers, the profession of my lips, nor any external symbols. It is the holy intention of the heart in prayer that counts.

I will pray the rosary continually for the intercession of the Blessed Virgin Mary. I will learn its crucifix, its beads, its promises, and its intentions. I will always keep it with me to pray in times of need, sorrow, and persecution. I will ever guard my rosary so that it becomes part of me. With my rosary I am a defender of the holy Catholic Faith. My rosary gives me mastery over demons and leads me to the Savior of my soul. I will pray the rosary until I hear the last trumpet sound and there is no eternal enemy left. Amen.[30]

Ten Reasons to Pray the Rosary

1. Say the rosary every day, to obtain peace for the world.

2. There is no surer means of calling down God's blessings upon the family than the daily recitation of the Rosary.

3. If families will but listen to my message and give Our Lady ten minutes of their twenty four hours by reciting the daily Family Rosary, I assure them that their homes will become, by God's grace, peace, prayerful places, little heavens, which God the Author of home life has intended they should be.

4. A powerful means of renewing our courage will undoubtedly be found in the Holy Rosary…"

5. We have elsewhere brought it to the attention of the devout Christian that not least among the advantages of the Rosary is the ready means it puts in his hands to nurture his faith, and to keep him from ignorance of his religion and the danger of error.

6. We do not hesitate to affirm again publicly that We put great confidence in the Holy Rosary for the healing of evils which afflict our times.

7. Therefore we are sure that Our children and all their brethren throughout the world will turn (the Rosary) into a school of learning for true perfection, as, with a deep spirit of recollection, they contemplate the teachings that shine forth from the life of Christ and of Mary Most Holy.

8. I think that I did not miss a single day in reciting it, including the most terrible times of battle when I had no rest night or day. How often did I see her manifest intercession in the decisions which I made in choosing a precise tactic. Take, then, the advice of an old soldier seasoned by experience: Do not neglect the recitation of the Rosary for any reason.

9. Among all the devotions approved by the Church none has been favored by so many miracles as the devotion of the Most Holy Rosary.

10. Those who say it fervently and frequently will gradually grow in grace and holiness and will enjoy the special protection of Our Lady and the abiding friendship of God. No one can live continually in sin and continue to say the Rosary—either he will give up sin or he will give up the Rosary. [31]

For Reflection

1. Why is the rosary such a powerful weapon against the forces of darkness?

2. How would you describe your relationship to Mary?

3. If you are willing, make a commitment to pray the rosary every day for the next month. Keep a journal of the difference this makes in your life and in the life of your family.

CHAPTER NINE

Called to Be a People of Hope

Blessed be the God and Father of our Lord Jesus Christ,
who has blessed us in Christ with every spiritual blessing
in the heavenly places, even as he chose us in him before
the foundation of the world, that we should be holy and
blameless before him. He destined us in love to be his sons
through Jesus Christ, according to the purpose of his will, to
the praise of his glorious grace which he freely bestowed on
us in the Beloved.

—Ephesians 1:3–6

We are called to be a people of hope, but one of the greatest weapons
the devil uses against us is discouragement. At times the sense of
discouragement can be so intense that it can paralyze you, making
you unable to take the next step. As Jesus said to St. Faustina:

> My child, know that the greatest obstacles to holiness are
> discouragement and an exaggerated anxiety. These will
> deprive you of the ability to practice virtue.... I am always
> ready to forgive you. As often as you beg for it, you glorify
> my mercy.[32]

Prayer and the sacraments are essential to deal with the attacks
of discouragement. We also need to take practical, natural steps.
Surround yourself with an environment that builds and supports
hope and encouragement. This includes the company you keep, the

entertainment you fill your mind with, and the way you care for your-self physically.

Remember, we are created body, mind, and soul. Each of these areas impacts the others to some degree. Others are counting on us to do what we can to be as healthy and faithful to God's design. God has called us to be instruments of hope and encouragement in our world.

> *Act of Hope*
> O my God, relying on your Almighty power and infinite mercy and promises, I hope to obtain pardon for my sins, the help of your grace, and life everlasting through the merits of Jesus Christ, my Lord and Redeemer, Amen.33

A Future Full of Hope

Jeremiah 29:11–14 tells us, "For I know the plans I have for you, says the Lord, plans for welfare and not for evil, to give you a future and a hope. Then you will call upon me and come and pray to me, and I will hear you. You will seek me and find me; when you seek me with all your heart. I will be found by you, says the Lord."

One of the most misunderstood and misused words in our vocabu-lary is the word *hope*. The reality of what this word means has been so watered down and distorted in our culture that few people under-stand its true meaning. The world gives us no hope—instead it tells us that we are hatched, matched, and dispatched; we are sprinkled with water, sprinkled with rice, and sprinkled with dirt. This is the atheistic, secular notion of "Eat, drink, and be merry, for tomorrow we die." Man's way leads to a *hopeless end*, while God's way leads to an *endless hope*.

Earthly hope disappoints us, but Christian hope does not disap-point. Real hope is built on a real faith, a solid, reasoned conviction that is awaiting the good things of our salvation in the experience of the present moment.

In everyday life people use the word *hope* this way: "I hope to see you soon," or, "I hope you feel better." These are just expressions of wishful thinking. This is *not* what the theological virtue of hope is all about. Pope Benedict XVI published an encyclical on the subject of hope, entitled *Spe Salvi*. The Holy Father opens the letter with this verse from St. Paul in Romans 8:24: "In hope we are saved."

The preceding verses tell how Paul considers the sufferings of the present as nothing compared to the glory that is to be ours. He says the whole world is waiting for the revelation of the Son of God. Paul clearly recognizes that there is pain, suffering, and evil in the world, but he tells us that it will be overcome if we believe in the Lord Jesus and his resurrection and live in the hope of our own resurrection. Our hope is in the Word, not in this world, and in the atoning work of Jesus Christ, and this hope, as Paul says, "does not disappoint us" (Romans 5:5).

Personally speaking, if hope were an investment, I would be a millionaire! Hope is what I give freely—hope in Jesus!

Staying Grounded in Hope

Since discouragement is so prevalent and easy to succumb to, how do we stay hopeful? This little acronym has helped me:

Humility

Obedience

Prayer

Eucharist

Hope is the natural result of being humble and obedient to God's will and making prayer and the Eucharist a priority. Above all, Jesus himself is our hope (see 1 Timothy 1:1). Christ in us is the reason for our hope; he is the promise now and for our future glory (see Colossians 1:27).

The Holy Spirit at Work in the World Brings Hope

The dramatic rise in lay movements in the twentieth and twenty-first century is another reason for hope. The Holy Spirit has been busy fostering many dynamic movements that are animating and equipping Catholics everywhere to be effective, Christ-centered apostles in the third millennium. This is a huge reason for hope. From the Militia of the Immaculata, founded by St. Maximilian Kolbe in 1917, and Legion of Mary in 1921 to FOCUS in 1998, with many, many others in between, the Holy Spirit's leading and presence is evident.

Each of these movements, communities, and apostolates has its own specific charism, its own mission. But the Holy the Spirit is the One who anoints and empowers each. These movements have been raised up, anointed, and empowered by the same Holy Spirit to fulfill a particular task in the Body of Christ. Pope John Paul II called these new movements "one of the most significant fruits of that springtime in the Church which was foretold by the Second Vatican Council."[34]

What common purposes do these ecclesial movements, communities, and apostolates share as members of the Body of Christ? Each is called to lead its adherents into greater holiness and to be witnesses of this call to holiness to others. Each is called to bring others to a personal encounter with Jesus Christ as Lord and Savior. Each is called to strengthen the faith of its adherents through proper catechesis. Each is called to live in communion with others in the body while living at the same time exercising each one's unique mission and charism. The principle of unity in diversity and diversity in unity must be the underlying attitude.

The re-evangelization of the Church primarily through the laity was predicted by Bishop Fulton J. Sheen, speaking to the Knights of Columbus in 1972. He said, "Who is going to save our Church? Not our bishops, not our priests and religious. It's up to *you*, the people."[35]

John Paul II also said this:

> The institutional and charismatic aspects are co-essential as it were to the Church's constitution. They contribute, although differently, to the life, renewal and sanctification of God's people. It is from this providential rediscovery of the Church's charismatic dimension that, before and after the Council, a remarkable pattern of growth has been established for ecclesial movements and new communities.[36]

Peace at Last

Let us take to heart and place our hope in the comforting words of Jesus:

> Let not your hearts be troubled; believe in God, believe also in me. In my Father's house are many rooms; if it were not so, would I have told you that I go to prepare a place for you? And when I go and prepare a place for you, I will come again and will take you to myself, that where I am you may be also. (John 14:1–3)

The Christian life is superior to all other ways of living—and I cannot overstate the advantage that the Christian will have for all eternity. Job said, "If a man die, shall he live again?" (14:14). He answered his own question when he said, "For I know that my Redeemer liveth, and in the last day, I shall rise out of the earth. And I shall be clothed again with my skin, and in my flesh I shall see my God" (Job

19:25–26, Douay-Rheims). Alleluia! One day we will rise from the grave (see John 6:53–56) and shout triumphantly, "Free at last! Free at last! Thank God Almighty I'm free at last!"

The great Southern Baptist preacher Billy Graham said this:

> The sea was beating against the rocks in huge, dashing waves. The lighting was flashing, the thunder was roaring, the wind was blowing; but the little bird was asleep in the crevice of the rock, its head serenely under its wing, sound asleep. That is peace: to be able to sleep in the storm! In Christ we are relaxed and at peace in the midst of the confusions, bewilderments, and perplexities of this life. The storm rages, but our hearts are at rest. We have found peace because we have learned to trust our living God![37]

For Reflection

Here is a helpful exercise suggested by Fr. John Hardon, S.J., on the virtue of hope.

1. Do I immediately say a short prayer when I find myself getting discouraged?
2. Do I daily say a short act of hope?
3. Do I dwell on my worries instead of dismissing them from my mind?
4. Do I fail in the virtue of hope by my attachment to the things of the world?
5. Do I try to see God's providence in everything that "happens" in my life?"
6. Do I try to see everything from the point of view of eternity?
7. Am I confident that, with God's grace, I will be saved?

8. Do I allow myself to worry about my past life, and thus weaken my hope in God's mercy?

9. Do I try to combine every fully deliberate action with at least a momentary prayer for divine help?

10. How often today have I complained, even internally? [38]

CHAPTER TEN

Dying for Jesus

Let us then cast off the works of darkness
and put on the armor of light.
—Romans 13:12

I started working for the Los Angeles County Sheriff's Department in 1981. I was assigned to the East Los Angeles Station (known as "Fort Apache") from 1988 to 1998 as a deputy sheriff. I was very active in police athletics—boxing, martial arts, and 10K races. Early on I learned that hard work garners the respect of one's peers, and I worked hard to earn the respect of my fellow deputies.

When a new crop of deputies was assigned to ELA Station, I recognized one of them: Johnny Martinez. He and I had worked together at the Men's Central Jail in downtown Los Angeles. It soon became obvious to me that Johnny was a fallen-away Catholic. In my evangelical Catholic mind, I knew that if I could reach him, he would be a strong ally in my efforts to evangelize my fellow deputies who were by and large lukewarm Catholics.

I began talking to Johnny every day about our Catholic faith as we were putting on our uniforms and getting ready to hit the streets. He had become focused on secular things and had lost his way. I could sense in our conversations that he was empty inside and looking for something greater than himself. I followed up my conversations with him by giving him cassette tapes on a variety of Catholic topics. He would come back the next day and ask me for another tape. Right before my eyes, he was getting intrigued and fired up day by day as

I shared my Catholic faith with him. In a matter of weeks he went to confession and attended Sunday Mass. Within a few months he began praying the rosary and reading his Bible daily, attending weekly adoration, and consecrating his life to Mary.

I saw Johnny Martinez go from an uneducated, lukewarm Catholic to a radioactive, contagious, evangelical Catholic who had fallen in love with God. Together we began evangelizing our fellow deputy sheriffs. The captain asked me one day, "What did you to Johnny? He has totally changed for the better. Whatever you did to him, I hope you can do it to the others—it would make my job so much easier." I told the captain that I simply invited Johnny to come back to his Catholic faith and open his heart to Jesus. He said, "Good man— keep it up."

Fast-forward about four years. Johnny and I were now working different shifts, so we didn't have much contact with each other. Johnny had a new partner, a trainee, and one Friday night they were just walking out of briefing and roll call when they got a 911-call: "22 Adam—245 shots fired—one person down, 22 Adam, code 3."

Johnny and his partner were less than a mile from the location, so Johnny responded and they sped off to the location in their black-and-white patrol car. They arrived within three minutes, and Johnny ordered his trainee partner to gather information from witnesses and put out a crime broadcast with the suspect(s) information to all patrol units in the area.

Johnny jumped out of the patrol car and ran over to tend to the victim prior to the paramedics arriving at the scene. He saw a male Hispanic in his late teens who had been shot several times in the torso with a semiautomatic handgun. Johnny recognized him as a notorious gang member named Mario, who was wanted on several felony warrants. Mario had been kicked out of several high schools in the East LA area and was on felony probation for a violent crime. Now he was on his back, riddled with bullets. The irony is that Mario was on probation for exactly the same crime: unloading a pistol on a rival gang member.

Deputy Martinez's initial thoughts and reactions were not very compassionate as he watched the teen crying and writhing in pain like a snake on the street. Johnny's first thought was, *Good—that's what he deserves, good old-fashioned street justice.* Then the Holy Spirit came over Johnny, and with moral clarity he thought, *Wait—what am I thinking? This guy is my prodigal brother in Christ, he may die in mortal sin, and I have to evangelize him.*

Johnny said he had a few seconds of cognitive dissonance; his spirit was fighting his very human thoughts, and he was struggling with whether Mario deserved *justice* or *mercy.* The Holy Spirit enabled Johnny to clearly see Mario with a renewed mind and a heart full of compassion. He experienced a word of knowledge from the Lord as he realized, *I am my brother's keeper.*

Johnny knelt alongside Mario, trying to comfort him with words while compressing a blanket on his torso to stop the flow of blood that was shooting out like a sprinkler every time Mario exhaled. The young man was in excruciating pain, panic-stricken and having a major meltdown. Johnny could see and hear the lights and siren of the paramedic unit about three blocks away. Deputy Martinez felt that Mario's life was ebbing away and so he asked him, "Mario, have you been baptized?" Mario said, "I don't know," so Johnny grabbed a bottle of water from one of the bystanders. He opened the bottle of water and poured it over Mario's head, saying, "I baptize you in the name of the Father and of the Son and of the Holy Spirit." Johnny then picked Mario up and cradled him in his arms, resembling the famous *Pieta* statue where the corpse of Jesus is cradled in Mary's arms. Apparently Johnny was not concerned for his own safety, coming in contact with somebody else's blood on the street with the accompanying risks for infectious diseases—he just wanted Mario to come in contact with the blood of Jesus so he would be forgiven and his soul saved.

Still holding Mario, Johnny began running towards the paramedics that were pulling up to the scene of the crime. All the while he was telling Mario, "Little brother, Jesus loves you! Repeat after me: 'Lord have mercy, Christ have mercy, Lord have mercy.'" Mario was gasping for air, but he repeated those words softly as his life was ebbing away. Johnny handed over Mario to the paramedics, and they sped away. Deputy Johnny Martinez stood there, covered in blood from the neck down and exhausted, not physically but emotionally. A few hundred onlookers witnessed this courageous act of Catholic evangelism in action, as well as several deputy sheriffs who had arrived at the scene.

Shortly after the incident, the ER doctor notified Johnny that Mario was pronounced dead at the hospital. This young man had never been evangelized or catechized. His father was doing a life sentence in the state prison for several homicide convictions, and his mother worked as a prostitute and waitress in Hollywood. The devil had plans to make Mario one of his disciples and then take him to hell, but God intervened. In his infinite goodness and mercy, he send Mario a messenger named Deputy Johnny Martinez who brought the saving waters of baptism, repentance and the love of Jesus Christ to a poor soul blinded by the world and walking in darkness.

Johnny and I have talked about this incident more than once, and we fully expect to see Mario on the other side one day in the New

Jerusalem, the streets of gold where God "will wipe away every tear from their eyes, and death shall be no more, neither shall there be mourning nor crying nor pain any more, for the former things have passed away. And he who sat upon the throne said, 'Behold, I make all things new'" (Revelation 21:4–5).

Those who believe in these promises are called Christians, and life's greatest joy is to be one. "Iron sharpens iron, and one man sharpens another" (Proverbs 27:17). Look at the way God works through us "unworthy servants" (Luke 17:10)—I evangelized Johnny, and Johnny evangelized Mario.

> Eternal rest grant unto Mario, O Lord, and let your perpetual light shine upon him. May his soul and the souls of all the faithfully departed through the mercy of God rest in peace. Amen.

For Reflection

1. While you may never face such a traumatic situation, who in your life might die without knowledge of the faith? What steps can you take to boldly witness to that person?
2. What opportunities have you had to share your faith in a work setting? How comfortable are you with doing so?
3. Have you had an experience where Christ's love suddenly replaced feelings of animosity and hatred? Describe what happened.

CHAPTER ELEVEN

He Is Risen!

In the most mysterious way God the Father has revealed his almighty power in the voluntary humiliation and resurrection of his Son, by which he conquered evil.... It is in Christ's resurrection and exaltation that the Father has shown forth "the immeasurable greatness of his power in us who believe."

—*CCC* 272

Unless we accept what the Scriptures teach about the resurrection, the entire Christian message virtually disintegrates. The whole preaching thrust of the apostolic age was based upon the fact that one quiet morning, in an obscure garden, one man had vanquished his most feared enemy, the vaunted angel of death. Satan had defeated the first Adam in a garden ages before, and with his victory there commenced the reign of sin and death over mankind. But now in God's appointed time and plan, Satan met the last Adam in still another garden, and death was "swallowed up in victory" (1 Corinthians 15:54).

Our Lord's resurrection is far more than just a proposition. It is the basic pillar upon which rests the hope of all Christians. St. Paul wrote, "And if Christ has not been raised, then our preaching is in van and your faith is in vain" (1 Corinthians 15:17). As Protestant apologist and evangelical minister Walter Martin wrote:

> The secular and scientific age in which we live demands that things be tested and re-tested. They require evidence upon evidence, fact upon fact. Yet here in the truest sense

is a controlled experiment. Christianity has been observed for almost two thousand years. Whenever it is faithfully proclaimed, accepted, and acted upon, it transforms men, cultures, and societies; and it can do this only because it is energized by a living Savior....

What was the central truth of the early apostles' preaching? What was the stimulus to the miraculous growth of the early Church? What was the energizing force which spread the gospel across the face of the earth? The answer to all these questions is the Resurrection of Jesus Christ. "He is risen!" was the victorious cry of the early Christians, and they spread it to the ends of the earth."[39]

Josh McDowell summed it up perfectly when he said, "I have come to the conclusion that the resurrection of Jesus Christ is one of the *most wicked, vicious, heartless hoaxes ever foisted upon the minds of men,* or it is the most fantastic fact of history."[40]

Jesus has three basic credentials: (1) the impact of his life upon history; (2) the fulfillment of prophecy in his life, and (3) his resurrection. The resurrection of Jesus Christ and Christianity stand or fall together.

The resurrection is the very keystone and central tenet of the Christian faith. When you compare Buddha, Confucius, Zoroaster, Mohammed, Gandhi, Aristotle, Plato, or Socrates to Jesus, the difference is time (mere men) and infinity (the God-man). Christianity is not fueled by fossils nor by the sages of science; rather, it is fueled by a living Savior. The babe from Bethlehem became the Christ on Calvary, and he has now become the Lord of the empty tomb.

The resurrection entered intimately into the life of the early Christians. Mention of the resurrection appears on their tombs and in the drawings found on the walls of the catacombs, and it entered deeply into early Christian hymnology. The resurrection became one of the great apologetic themes in the writings of the first four centuries; it was the constant focal point of the early Church Fathers' preaching, and it became part of the great creeds of the Catholic Church.

Here is a sample of what the early Fathers had to say regarding the resurrection:

> He was crucified in reality, and not in appearance, not in imagination, not in deceit. He really died, and was buried, and rose from the dead, even as He prayed in a certain place, saying, "But do Thou, O Lord, raise me up again, and I shall recompense them." And the Father, who always hears Him, answered and said, "Arise, O God, and judge the earth; for Thou shall receive all the heathen for Thine inheritance." The Father, therefore, who raised Him up, will also raise us up through Him, apart from whom no one will attain to true life. (Ignatius of Antioch)[41]

> For since the Lord went away into the midst of the shadow of death where the souls of the dead were, and afterwards arose in the body, and after the resurrection was taken up, it is clear that the souls of his disciples, on account of which the Lord underwent these things, will go away into the place allotted to them by God.[42] (St. Irenaeus)

> We believe that He suffered and that, in accord with the Scriptures, He died and was buried; and that He was raised again by the Father to resume His place in heaven, sitting at the right of the Father. (Tertullian)[43]

By whom all things were made, both which be in heaven and in earth. Who for us men and for our salvation came down [from heaven] and was incarnate and was made man. He suffered and the third day he rose again, and ascended into heaven. And he shall come to judge the quick and the dead. (From the Creed of Nicaea, 325 A.D.)[44]

After this, we acknowledge the resurrection of the dead, of which Jesus Christ our Lord became the firstling; who bore a body not in appearance but in truth, derived from Mary the Mother of God. (Bishop Alexander of Alexandria)[45]

In *Who Moved the Stone?*, a book which has become a classic, Frank Morrison, a lawyer, tells us how he had been brought up in a rationalistic environment, and had come to the opinion that the account of the resurrection was nothing but a fairy tale happy ending which spoiled the matchless story of Jesus. Therefore, he planned to write an account of the last tragic days of Jesus, allowing the full horror of the crime and the full heroism of Jesus to shine through. He would, of course, omit any suspicion of the miraculous, and would utterly discount the resurrection. But when it came to study the facts with care, he had to change his mind. As Lee Strobel writes in the foreword to the 1958 edition:

The more he let his conclusions take him unhindered to where the evidence pointed, the more he became stunned by his findings. The outcome proved to be quite different from what he anticipated. In the end, he came to believe there is "a deep and profoundly historical basis for that much disputed sentence in the Apostles' Creed—"the third day he rose again from the dead." His findings…quickly became a powerful testimony to the evidence for the resurrection of Jesus.[46]

In the *Handbook of Christian Apologetics*,[47] authors Dr. Peter Kreeft and Fr. Ronald Taceli state five possible theories for Christ's resurrection: (1) Christianity; (2) hallucination; (3) myth; (4) conspiracy; and (5) swoon. Of these theories, four are non-believing theories. I'd like to look at them in reverse order—from the simplest, least popular, and most easily refuted to the most confusing, most popular, and most difficult to refute—and then share the logic that Kreeft and Taceli use to explain the rational basis for the resurrection.

Swoon
This theory says that Jesus didn't really die; he just was in a "swoon," a coma-like state from which he eventually woke up. It's fairly easy to dismiss this theory. First of all, Jesus could not have survived the crucifixion. The fact that the Roman soldiers didn't break Jesus's legs meant that they thought Jesus was most likely dead already. The fact that John saw water and blood coming from Jesus's side shows that Jesus's lungs had collapsed, causing him to die of asphyxiation. This is a medical certainty.

Jesus's post-resurrection appearances convinced the apostles that he was vitally and gloriously alive. If Jesus had merely struggled back to consciousness after a swoon, he would have been badly in need of medical attention. A weak, staggering sick man who is barely alive is not someone who comes across as the divine Lord of all who has conquered death. And how would the Roman guards at the tomb have been overpowered by a swooning shell of a man who had been tightly wrapped in sheets and entombed? Lastly, could someone newly awakened from a swoon be able to move the huge stone at the opening of the tomb? If not, who moved it if not an angel?

Conspiracy

This theory argues that the disciples made up the whole story about the resurrection. It just doesn't seem likely that the disciples would go to such lengths to concoct such a story. If they made up the story, these fishermen were the most creative, clever, intelligent charlatans in history. The character of the disciples provides an argument strongly against such a conspiracy These were simple, honest, common peasants, not conniving liars. Their sincerity is proved by their words and deeds. They preached a resurrected Christ and they lived a resurrected Christ. They willingly died for their conspiracy. Nothing proves sincerity like martyrdom.

The change of their lives from fear to faith, despair to confidence, confusion to certitude, runaway cowardice to steadfast boldness under threat of persecution not only proves their sincerity but testifies to some kind of powerful cause behind it. Imagine twelve poor, fearful, uneducated, peasants changing the hard-nosed Roman world with a lie.

Hallucination

If you thought you saw a dead man walking and talking, you might think you were hallucinating. It's not so far-fetched that disciples might have been hallucinating, is it?

However, there were too many witnesses. Hallucinations are private, individual, and subjective. The risen Christ appeared to Mary Magdalene, the apostles, the two disciples on the road to Emmaus, the fishermen on the shore, and a crowd of more than five hundred at once (see 1 Corinthians 15:6) St. Paul says that most of the five hundred people were still alive, inviting any reader to check the truth of the story by questioning the eyewitnesses. He could never have done this and gotten away with it, given the power, resources, and numbers of his enemies, if it were not true. And it would be highly unlikely that such a group hallucination would have taken place.

Hallucinations usually happen only once to a person, unless that person is insane. This hallucination recurred many times, to ordinary people (see John 20:19—21:14; Acts 1:3). Another thing about hallucinations: They usually last a few seconds or minutes—rarely hours. This one hung around for forty days (see Acts 1:3).

Initially, even the apostles thought he was a ghost, and Jesus had to eat something to prove that he wasn't (see Luke 24:36–43). The disciples were also able to touch him and carry on conversations with him.

Myth

The style of the Gospels is radically and clearly different from the typical style of myths throughout history. There are no overblown, spectacular, childishly exaggerated events in the Gospels. A second refuting of the myth theory is that there wasn't enough time for a myth to develop; eyewitnesses to Jesus and the events of the passion were still alive who could be questioned as to the validity of the resurrection.

The myth theory has two layers. The first layer is that the historical Jesus was not divine, did not claim divinity, performed no miracles, and did not rise from the dead. The second layer is the Gospels as we have them, with a Jesus who claimed to be divine, performed miracles, and rose from the dead. There is not any evidence for the first part of the theory, since we have no other story than the one handed down to us than the one contained in the Gospels. The letters of early Christian writers (such as Barnabas, Clement, Irenaeus, Polycarp, Ignatius, and Justin) speak of the resurrection, and most of these men were descendants of the apostles.

For the myth theory to be true, the validity of the entire New Testament would need to be questioned. But in essence, Christianity does not invalidate the myth theory—it validates them by incarnating them. The historical evidence alone is massive enough to convince the open-minded inquirer. Compared with any other historical event, the resurrection has eminently credible evidence behind it. To disbelieve it, we must make an exception to the rules we use everywhere else in history.

The resurrection of Christ is not just an Easter-time phenomenon to be celebrated in song and service—it is literally the dawn of every new day of our lives. Because Christ lives, the Scriptures say, we will live, too! (John 14:19). The crucifix demonstrates God's full love; the resurrection demonstrates God's full power. He is risen—Alleluia!

For Reflection

1. Was there a time in your life that you struggled with the idea of Jesus's resurrection? Describe how you came to believe that Jesus truly rose from the dead.

2. How does Christ's resurrection affect your life today?

3. Do you see yourself as risen in Christ? What does this really mean?

CHAPTER TWELVE

A Band of Brothers

How good and pleasant it is when brothers
dwell together in unity!
—Psalm 133:1

Here's an insight for us that God the Father gave to St. Catherine of Siena on the inherent incompleteness of our design and our clear need for others in the general reality of spiritual growth:

> The same is true of many of my gifts and graces, virtues and other spiritual gifts, and those things necessary for the body and human life. I have distributed them all in such a way that no one has all of them. Thus I have given you reason—necessity, in fact—to practice mutual charity. For I could well have supplied you with all your needs, both spiritual and material. But I wanted to make you dependent on one another...[48]

This chapter is specifically directed to my male readers, who might appreciate some insights on the value of building relationships with their Christian brothers. I am part of a men's fellowship that meets every Monday night at my church. Our mutual purpose is to grow in virtue and holiness. We also constantly remind each other about the importance of examining our conscience daily. As the Bible says:

> Why should a living man complain,
> a man, about the punishment of his sins!

> Let us test and examine our ways,
>
> and return to the Lord! (Lamentations 3:39–40)

> Let a man examine himself... (1 Corinthians 11:28)

Our group is called the Brotherhood of St. Dismas, and it's one of three such groups in California. St. Dismas was the "good thief" mentioned in Luke 23:29. After a life of rebellion against God, he found himself dying on a cross next to Jesus. His sorrow for his sins was so great and his faith in Christ so strong that our Lord promised to bring him to paradise that very day. We chose St. Dismas as our patron because his example inspires us to trust in God's mercy, hope for our own salvation, and turn away from sin.

To help each other achieve these goals, we focus on six areas: meeting together, weekly fasting, praying the rosary daily and petitioning St. Dismas, spiritual reading and time before the Blessed Sacrament, evangelization, and striving to set a good example and offend no one.

As we examine our consciences, we ask ourselves the following questions:

1. Have I missed weekly meetings or failed to attend functions of the Brotherhood? Proverbs 13:20 says, "He who walks with wise men becomes wise, but the companion of fools will suffer harm," and Hebrews 10:24–25 tells us, "Let us consider how to stir up one another to love and good works, not neglecting to meet together, as is the habit of some, but encouraging one another."

Ecclesiastes 4:9–12 points out how valuable it is to have support and help from others: "Two are better than one, because they have a good reward for their toil. For if they fall, one will lift up his fellow; but woe to him who is alone when he falls and has not another to lift him up. Again, if two lie together, they are warm; but how can one be warm alone? And though a man might prevail against one who is alone, two will withstand him. A threefold cord is not quickly broken."

One way to cause a fire to burn out is to pull the logs apart. We've learned that if we pull apart from each other, our fire will go out, individually and collectively. As Proverbs 27:17 tells us: "Iron sharpens iron, and one man sharpens another."

2. Have I fulfilled our common penances of weekly fasting and abstinence from meat? Penance, as defined by Fr. John Hardon in the *Catholic Dictionary,* is "punishment by which one atones for sins committed, either by oneself or by others." It's interesting to note that the word *penitentiary* comes from the word *penitence,* which is where we get the word *penance.* Prison originally was supposed to be a time of doing external works of sacrifice to demonstrate that one was sorry for one's crimes and sins. Fasting is a form of penance, and our group has chosen to fast one day per week. Every Friday we eat one full meatless meal, with the other two meals not equaling one full meal.

Fr. John Hardon, S.J., defined abstinence as "the moral virtue that inclines a person to the moderate use of food or drink as dictated by right reason or by faith for his own moral and spiritual welfare."[49]

3. Have I prayed the rosary daily and included my petition to St Dismas? The Blessed Mother promises her special protection and greatest graces to those who pray a daily rosary. She told St. Dominic back in the twelfth century that the rosary is powerful armor against the forces of hell: The rosary destroys vice, decreases sin, and defeats heresies. Mary says that praying the rosary causes good works to flourish, along with virtue. This kind of armor was needed back in the twelfth century and it's definitely needed today![50]

4. Have I done my spiritual reading and spent time before the Blessed Sacrament? It's so important to fill your mind with good spiritual material, and often the perfect time to do this kind of reading is before the Blessed Sacrament. This is a weekly commitment that pays incredible dividends. Just as you can't be exposed to the sun without receiving its rays, neither can you be exposed to Jesus in the Blessed Sacrament without receiving the divine rays of his grace, his love, and his peace. "Christ is truly Emmanuel, which means 'God with us.' For He is in the midst of us day and night. He dwells in us with the fullness of grace and of truth."[51]

5. Have I neglected to evangelize others when I had the opportunity? Pope Leo XIII said, "The first law of history is not to dare to utter falsehood; the second, not to fear to speak the truth."[52] And St. Paul wrote to Timothy: "Do your best to present yourself to God as one approved, a workman who has no need to be ashamed, rightly handling the word of truth" (2 Timothy 2:15). We should look for opportunities to share our faith—boldly and respectfully—with those around us. A chance encounter might have eternal ramifications for someone who crosses our path, if we are equipped and ready to share.

6. Have I offended another brother or been a bad example? The *Catechism* tells us that scandal is "an attitude or behavior which leads another to do evil. The person who gives scandal becomes his neighbor's tempter. He damages virtue and integrity; he may even draw his brother into spiritual death. Scandal is a grave offense if by deed or omission another is deliberately led into a grave offense" (*CCC*, 2284). We must always walk circumspectly, never intentionally being a stumbling block to someone else. And if we do offend a brother, we can do all within our power to make things right.

After we read and reflect on that week's Scripture, we discuss questions that the leader for that week has prepared ahead of time. This group has been instrumental in my own spiritual growth; there's just nothing like knowing you are part of a tight-knit brotherhood who are all seeking to love God and others to the best of their ability under the power of the Holy Spirit.

We end our time with the following prayer:

> Heavenly Father, we ask you to hear our prayers, to bless and protect us and our brothers who are absent, to remember those who are incarcerated, to increase our brotherhood, and to have mercy on the souls of the faithful departed. We ask this in the name of our Lord, Jesus Christ, and through the intercession of the Blessed Virgin, and our holy patron St. Dismas.

A Man's Mission

A priest once told me that every man has a *mission*, an *identity* and a *journey*. As men, our natural mission is to be *leaders, protectors, and providers*. Our supernatural mission is to be *priests, prophets, and kings*.

A man's identity is meant to progress from a *beloved son* to a *loyal brother* to a *vital ma*n. Once he is an adult, he typically becomes a *devoted husband*, then a *strong father*, and finally a *veteran sage*. A man's journey is designed by God to lead his family, in virtue and by example, to their final destination: heaven.

Jesus Christ is our perfect role model. He is the Lamb of God (who suffered and died for us). He is also the Lion of Judah (who will come back one day to take us to heaven and destroy evil). Every Catholic woman wants a man who demonstrates being a lamb by his sacrificial love, and she wants a lion to lead her from this world into the next. This is her "Prince Charming."

My Catholic men's group helps me *stay on course;* it helps guide me on this pilgrimage to heaven and to holiness. Why is it so important for men to meet together regularly? Here are ten reasons, which I learned from Maurice Blumberg, the founding executive director for the National Fellowship of Catholic Men:

Why Men Need Each Other

- Because we are social beings who need the companionship of other men
- To help one another sort through the current confusion about masculinity and manliness
- To gain a more balanced perspective on life
- To help one another grow and develop in our roles as husbands, fathers, and Christian workers through the give-and-take of trusted relationships between brothers in Christ
- To relieve the strain men can put on their wives to satisfy all their emotional and social needs
- To enhance each other's ability to make wise decisions about critical areas affecting major aspects of life
- To help each other through the difficult circumstances and suffering that are part of being human, such as the death of a family member or serious illness
- To better serve the Lord, grow in personal holiness, bear fruit for God's kingdom, and be a sign of Christ's love to others
- To help fight worldly temptations, overcome sinful habits, and protect one another from attacks of the world, the flesh, and the devil
- To help each other grow in our relationship with Jesus and experience more deeply God's love for us.[53]

Men can sometimes forget that relationships with other men are important. I would encourage all Catholic men to seek other men who share your faith and who have some common interests. They may be fellow parishioners, coworkers, or neighbors. Begin meeting regularly for prayer, study, and fellowship. You will be surprised at what God can do through a small group of Catholic men who love him and love one another. For me, my men's group ultimately is helping me *become the best version of myself.*

Remember, a real brother walks *with* you when the rest of the world walks *on* you.

For Reflection

For men...

1. Do you feel comfortable meeting with other men to discuss spiritual things? If not, what makes you uncomfortable? Do you see how being accountable to others might help you grow spiritually?

2. How important are your male friendships? Do you make your friends a priority, or are you content with work relationships or casual acquaintances?

3. Think of one of your closest friends. What do you value most about this person?

CHAPTER THIRTEEN

Evangelizing a Juvenile Delinquent

My brothers, if any one among you wanders from the truth and some one brings him back, let him know that whoever brings back a sinner from the error of his way will save his soul from death and will cover a multitude of sins.

—James 5:19

Back in the mid 1990s, I was working the day shift on a Friday in East Los Angeles. I received a radio dispatch to go to Humphrey Park where the park personnel had detained a juvenile who had skipped school and was smoking pot and writing graffiti in the park's restroom. When I got there, I took custody of this juvenile, whose name was Juan, handcuffing him and escorting him to my squad car. I informed him that he was being arrested for truancy, vandalism, possession of marijuana, and being under the influence.

As we drove to the jail I began asking him about his parents. He told me that he was an orphan from Mexico who had been in Los Angeles for two or three years, being bounced from one foster home to another. He told me that he didn't know anybody he could trust or that he considered a friend. I told Juan that I had a best friend that could be trusted with anything. I asked him if he would like to meet my best friend, and Juan said yes.

I said, "Jesus is my best friend. Whenever you are afraid, or tempted to do something bad, talk to him. He loves you; he cares for you more than anybody else."

Juan began to get teary-eyed, which is quite unusual for a street kid because they pride themselves on being rough and tough. I began telling him that God was his true father and Mary his real mother. I told him he was my little brother in the family of God. Juan became overwhelmed with joy. I asked him to pray with me, and he agreed. I took out a rosary from my pocket and led him in the Chaplet of Divine Mercy. He prayed along with me, weeping the whole time. I placed my hands on his head and blessed him, just the way I bless my own children with the Sign of the Cross. He cried like a baby.

I told him it was time to go to the jail. I put the handcuffs on him and put him in the patrol car, and we began driving to the jail. From the backseat of my patrol car, Juan told me, "Deputy Romero, I have never felt so much love in my whole life like I did inside that church. I wanted you to handcuff me to the pew so I could never leave. I never felt so much peace in my life as I have today after talking with you." Tears continued to roll down his eyes.

We pulled into the sheriff's station parking lot, and when I opened the back door, I noticed that Juan was still very emotional. I took out my handkerchief and wiped away his tears. I gave him a prayer card with the words of the *Anima Christi* prayer, and I told him to pray that prayer every morning and evening so he could have a personal relationship with Jesus. He responded, "Thank you, Deputy, I will, I promise. I want to know Jesus like you do!" I then walked him inside the jail to book him in for his crimes.

Was this encounter by coincidence? No, our heavenly Father prepared this encounter—this was divine providence at work in both of our lives.

Passive or Passionate

Now let me ask *you*: Why are you here? What is your purpose? Are Catholics meant to live out a passive existence in this life while we wait to die and go to heaven? Or is there something more? The Bible tells us in Genesis 1:28 that God created us to multiply, fill the earth, and take dominion of his creation for his glory. When Jesus came to earth, he gave his disciples the Great Commission, telling them to make disciples of all nations (see Matthew 28:18–20). These two mandates form the basis for why Christ's Church exists on this planet.

Every square inch of this world belongs to Christ the King. It is our privilege to serve him by exercising dominion in every area of life and serving wayward children like Juan. We are not meant to wander through our days, passive and directionless. Every life has a purpose—what is yours? If you don't know the answer, it's time to wake up! Whatever else you do in life, your baptismal duty is to evangelize (see 2 Timothy 4:5).

Jesus Christ came to save the lost, the least, and the last. Catholic evangelization is the very reason why the Church exists; it's our birthright, our great missionary call, our vocation, our great treasure. It is the pearl of great price that we want to share with the world. The New Evangelization is our responsibility! If not us than who? If not now, when?

My motto is: Trust God. Save Souls. Slay Error.

For Reflection

1. Do you see yourself playing a role in seeking and saving the lost, or is this something for pastors and missionaries? What part could God be calling you to play?

2. How passionate are you when it comes to your relationship with Jesus Christ? Do you consider him your best friend?

3. Are there any areas of passivity where living your faith is concerned? What might you do to turn those into passion?

CHAPTER FOURTEEN

Sin and Mercy–The Story of David and Bathsheba

Create in me a clean heart, O God,
and put a new and right spirit within me.
—Psalm 51:10

The story of David and Bathsheba (beginning in 2 Samuel 11) contains a lesson for all of us. It's a moving example of the consequences of sin and selfishness, and it contains a powerful message of mercy and forgiveness for those who are contrite and humble.

Taking place about a thousand years before the birth of Jesus, it's a rag-to-riches story of a shepherd boy who becomes king and his remarkable military success—which stemmed from his personal friendship with God and his obedience to God's will. In 2 Samuel 11:1, everything is going well for David—so well that he no longer leads his troops in battle. Instead, he has a trusted general, Joab, who can lead the attack on the Ammonites' capital city, Rabbah.

With his troops on the battlefield and little to do, David takes a walk late one afternoon along the parapets of his palace overlooking much of the city, and there below him he sees a beautiful women bathing. David already has many wives, but he is used to power and having whatever he wants. David's lust for this woman leads him to commit adultery with her. When she tells him that she is pregnant, David attempts to avoid the potential disgrace by arranging the murder of her husband, Uriah.

He summons Uriah home from the war, supposedly to bring him news from the battlefield, but really David is giving him an opportunity to sleep with his wife and claim paternity of the child in Bathsheba's womb. Uriah, however, is honorable; he knows that as a soldier for Israel on a mission of war, he is expected to stay away from women, even his own wife. Next David tries to get him drunk, but Uriah still refrained from going to his own house. Now David knows he is going to get caught, so he has Uriah take a letter to General Joab—a letter that contains the orders for Uriah's own death! David instructs Joab to position Uriah on the frontlines during an especially dangerous attack on the walls of Rabbah, and sure enough, Uriah was slaughtered by the Ammonites.

When Bathsheba learns of Uriah's death, she mourns for her husband, but when the time of mourning is over, David marries her. It sure looks like he has gotten away with adultery and murder…but he forgot one thing: God sees everything. The Lord sends Nathan the prophet to confront David with his sin. David felt the sting of Nathan's words and he confessed his sin. Nathan assures him of God's forgiveness, but he warns him that there will still be severe consequences. After this, David wrote Psalm 51, a prayer for cleansing and pardon, a prayer of repentance. He is honest about his sinfulness, and begs God to have mercy on him and cleanse him. "Create in me a clean heart, O God, and put a new and right spirit within me" (Psalm 51:10). He asks God to restore the joy of his salvation, and he promises to teach other sinners God's ways so they can return to him.

God's mercy truly is greater than his justice; however, just as Nathan warned, David still had to experience the consequences of his sins. And these consequences did not only affect David himself—they extended down through several generations! We don't realize how impactful our choices can be in the lives of others! In David's case, two of his sons died (one was killed by another of David's sons,

Absalom), and then Absalom revolted against David, seizing his throne and publicly insulting him by sleeping with David's wives where all in Israel could see. Finally Absalom dies too, in a battle between his troops and David's. And then, Adonijah, David's fourth son, is put to death by Solomon for trying to usurp David's throne.

God consoled David by blessing him with his son Solomon, who would succeed him on the throne. And because of David's contrite heart, God granted David military victory over his enemies.

God's Mercy

Was King David forgiven? Bear in mind that he had just committed several extremely grievous sins, deceit, adultery, and murder! David truly repented, before God and all Israel. But God still was extremely angry and disappointed beyond measure. Could he forgive? Would he forgive? Should he forgive? If there's one divine trait we humans should never forget, it's God's mercy. The God of Abraham, Isaac, and Jacob is a merciful Being; His mercy endures for all eternity.

King David was forgiven. His deep repentance and cry for mercy stirred the heart of Almighty God and God forgave him. And while he still had to suffer because of his actions, Acts 13:22 calls him "a man after [God's] own heart."

But how can we say that David's sin was forgiven if so many terrible things happened as a consequence of that sin? Consider this: The main consequence of David's blatant sin was eternal death! When David repented, that sentence of eternal death was revoked. But the repercussions, the here-and-now results, of David's sin still remained. Like an ugly scar that remains long after a deep wound has healed, those repercussions continued. What lessons can we learn from these events? How about:

God punishes blatant sin. It doesn't matter whether one is a king or a commoner—sin is always punished by God, and its effects often are felt even three or four generations later!

God's mercy is everlasting. Mercy is one of God's best-known traits, and it endures forever! Read Psalm 136—each of its twenty-six verses ends with the words "for his mercy endures for ever."

Always remember: If we sin and then repent—truly repent like King David did—then our Almighty God and Father will surely forgive us.

For Reflection

1. Do you see any correlation between your health and your holiness? Describe.
2. How would you describe God's mercy to someone else?
3. Can you remember a time when you experienced God's forgiveness—as well as the consequences for your poor choices?

CHAPTER FIFTEEN

A Muslim Taxi Driver Hears the Truth

For the weapons of our warfare are not worldly but have
divine power to destroy strongholds.
—2 Corinthians 10:4

I have been preaching the Catholic gospel for decades. I have spoken in well over a thousand Catholic churches, traveling to virtually every state in this country. Most of my parish evangelization missions are uneventful. I fly to a location, I get picked up at an airport, I'm taken to the church to speak, and I'm driven to a hotel at the end of the night. I'm picked up the next day to continue the parish mission, I am taken out to dinner and then dropped off at the airport. I get a lot of reading and praying done at the airport and on the plane, and once I get to Los Angeles, I hop into my car and drive home. I love my life, I love what I do, and I wake up every morning with a sense of purpose and mission.

I want to be the kind of man that when my feet hit the floor each morning the devil says "Uh-oh, he's up!" Life is too short to wake up with regrets. Therefore, love the people who treat you right. Forgive the ones who don't—just because you can. Believe that everything happens for a reason (see Romans 8:28). If you get a second chance, grab it with both hands. If it changes your life, let it. Take a few minutes to think before you act when you're mad. God never said life would be easy; he just promised it would be worth it.

What is the purpose of life? *Life is preparation for eternity—that's the bottom line.* We were made to last forever, and God wants us to be with him in heaven forever. One day my heart is going to stop, and that will be the end of my body—but not the end of my soul. I may live sixty to a hundred years on earth, but I am going to spend trillions of years in eternity. This life is just the warm-up—the dress rehearsal. God wants us to practice on earth what we will do forever in eternity, and that is to love.

The Adventure Begins

In February 2007 I flew from Los Angeles to Milwaukee to speak at the first annual Catholic Men's Conference, which was being held in an arena in West Bend, Wisconsin. The organizers were expecting about 1,000 men, but they ended up with about 2,500 men—the Holy Spirit was all over this conference. I flew in on Friday night, and I was able to go to confession and do a Holy Hour that evening with a rosary in one hand, my Bible in the other, and Jesus right in front of me in the tabernacle!

When I woke up on Saturday morning I said my morning prayers, went to morning Mass, and received my Lord in the Holy Eucharist. Boy oh boy, I was ready for battle. As Pope Paul VI said:

> In the earthly liturgy, by way of foretaste, we share in that heavenly liturgy which is celebrated in the holy city of Jerusalem toward which we journey as pilgrims, where Christ is sitting at the right hand of God.... We sing a hymn to the Lord's glory with all the warriors of the heavenly army...[54]

St. Catherine of Siena said that when you are one with God, you love what God loves and hate what he hates. She went on to say:

> This gives them such strength that nothing can harm them. They act like true knights who never consider any rising storm

so great that they are daunted by it. They have no fear because it is not in themselves that they trust. No, all their faith and trust is in God, whom they love, because they see that he is strong, and that he is willing and able to help them."[55]

Thus fortified, I headed over to the conference to listen to the morning speakers. Some were laymen like myself, and others were priests. The Holy Spirit had anointed all of them, and the truth was being preached and proclaimed with power. This was "muscular Christianity" at its best. I was scheduled to speak right after lunch at 2:00 p.m., and I would have an hour to present my topic. I went to the adoration chapel at about 1:00 p.m. with my rosary, and I began praying to Our Lady.

As I prayed, I meditated on Mary, who crushed the head of the serpent (see Genesis 3:15), and I reflected on a verse of Scripture that I had heard was a reference to the Blessed Virgin Mary:

Who is this that looks forth like the dawn, fair as the moon, bright as the sun, terrible as an army with banners? (Song of Solomon 6:10)

A volunteer came to call me from the adoration chapel and remind me that I was on in about fifteen minutes. In my deputy sheriff days, before I went on duty, I would go to a briefing or roll call. Today, my "briefing" before going "on duty" takes place in Adoration chapels around the country where I get my S.W.A.T. training: Spiritual Weapons And Tactics. Law Enforcement agencies around the country employ what is known as COPS (Community Oriented Policing Services). The Catholic Church through baptism gives me the same COPS mandate: Christians Obediently Preaching Salvation.

I mounted the stage and took the microphone. I opened up with prayer and then spoke to the men about God's Divine Mercy. I delivered my message with the energy and conviction that has become my trademark. I am a pyromaniac for Jesus! I'm a straight shooter—I shoot straight for the heart! My message is a no-nonsense, no-spin, Bible-centered, Holy Spirit, firebrand Catholicism.

An Eventful Ride

Right after my talk, I had to leave for the airport because I was scheduled to speak the next day at a Hispanic men's conference in downtown Los Angeles. A taxi pulled up in front of the arena, I bid farewell to my brothers in Christ, and we drove off. The first thing I noticed was that the taxi driver had recognizable prison tattoos on his neck and his arms. I immediately knew that he was a parolee who had done time in prison and was affiliated with a white prison gang.

Nonetheless, he was pleasant, and we began to talk. He told me that we had a thirty-minute drive to the airport. He asked me what brought me to the West Bend Wisconsin's sports arena. I told him that I was a Catholic evangelist that gave motivational talks to Catholic audiences. He was fascinated. He told me to call him Tom, and I told him to call me Jess. I was wearing a large St. Benedict medal around my neck, and I could see him looking at it through the rearview mirror.

Tom began asking me probing yet serious questions about the Catholic faith. He was surprised to hear that there are laypeople like myself who are married and preach the Gospel as a vocation. Tom told me that he thought of evangelists as being Protestants, not Catholics. After ten or fifteen minutes, I told Tom I was impressed with his line of questioning, and I asked him if he was Catholic. Suddenly the tone of his voice changed, and he said, "No, I used to be Catholic, but now I'm a Muslim."

I put the pieces together in my mind quickly. Tom was around my age, so he might have been a cultural Catholic who had never been properly catechized or evangelized. Maybe he had a poorly formed conscience. My guess was that Tom became a crook and/or a doper; he landed in prison, joined a white prison gang for protection, and was subsequently proselytized by Muslim prisoners. I asked Tom if he would share his faith journey with me—I wanted to know how and why he left Catholicism for Islam.

Tom told me that he liked the discipline and the militancy found within Islam. He said that Mohammed was a man's man—a man of war and Allah's final prophet on earth. He told me he liked Islam for three reasons:

He promised all faithful Muslim men seventy-two virgins in the afterlife.

Muslims are not required to forgive your enemy; instead, you can smite, strike, and kill your enemy.

There is no separation of religion and government.

He told me that Mohammed was the perfect man, while Jesus was pathetically weak and not the true Son of Allah (the name for God in Islam) because Allah has no son. He shared that Islam represents strength while Christianity represents weakness. Then Tom—as if possessed by a demon—went into a two-minute blasphemous diatribe against the Lord Jesus Christ.

I took a deep breath. I was stewing inside; you could have boiled an egg on my head. The intellectual side of me wanted to let him have it, but the faith-filled side of me called upon the Holy Spirit for peace and wisdom, so I could offer Tom *reasons for our faith in Christ*. I figured that I would speak the truth in love as best I could (see Ephesians 4:15). I began to share with Tom what I knew of how Jesus compared with Mohammed:[56]Tom the taxi driver looked as if he was ready to explode. His jaw was clenched, the veins in his neck were popping out, and he was hyperventilating. Clearly he was reacting strongly to hearing the truth. Immediately I thought of the Scripture: "A fool gives full vent to his anger, but a wise man quietly holds it back" (Proverbs 29:11). I saw that we were about ten minutes away from the airport.

Tom responded by saying, "So you're a Catholic evangelist, preaching around the country. Well, let me tell you what I feel like doing to you right now. I feel like killing you—and then I will go straight to paradise for killing an infidel." Tom went on to say that he was going to drive the car off the road, crashing it on purpose in order to kill me.

My lower nature threatened to kick in again. Suddenly, though, I felt the Holy Spirit's power, and I was flooded with a deep peace and a sense of excitement. I began to think, *What am I afraid of? I have Jesus, and if I die for standing up for him, I will be a martyr and go straight to heaven. Lord, are you choosing me right now—is this the way my life is going to end? Whatever pain I'll feel from a fatal car crash will last a few minutes or a few seconds, and then I will be with Jesus in heaven—Alleluia!*

But then, my mind flashed back to California. I thought about my beloved wife Anita, and my children, Paul, Annmarie, and Joshua back at home. What if I never saw them again? I felt comforted by God's promise that he would be a "Father of the fatherless and a protector of widows" (Psalm 68:5–6).

I had no doubt that Tom was going to carry out his threat any second—we were the only car on the road. Tom probably thought I was going to start begging for my life, or retract everything I said about Mohammed, or even deny my faith. A wise saying came to my mind: "A coward dies a thousand deaths, a courageous valiant person only dies once." The Holy Spirit gave me a verse: "Do not fear, only believe" (Mark 5:36). I decided that if Tom the taxi driver killed me, he would have to kill me proclaiming the name of Jesus.

I grabbed my St Benedict's medal and said the words of the Emperor Constantine before the Battle of the Milvian Bridge: *"In Hoc Signo Vinces"* (In this sign you will conquer). I said a silent, deeply felt Act of Contrition in case I was lacking humility and charity, and then I leaned forward a few inches from Tom's ear and spoke firmly and clearly. "Go ahead and crash the car. You're not talking to some boy; I'm ready to die—are you? I know my Savior, and his name is Jesus."

I knew that I was in a state of grace and that my soul was ready for death. I told him that if he crashed the car, he would see my soul separate from my mangled body and be received by my Lord Jesus Christ and taken into heaven. I asked him, "Tom, where will your soul go?"

Tom seemed angrier than ever. I began repeating John 6:53–56 a few inches from his ear: "Truly, truly, I say to you, unless you eat the flesh of the Son of man and drink his blood, you have no life in you: he who eats my flesh and drinks my blood has eternal life, and I will raise him up at the last day. For my flesh is food indeed, and my blood is drink indeed. He who eats my flesh and drinks my blood abides in me, and I in him." Although Tom seemed angrier than ever, he didn't drive off the road and we arrived at the airport.

As we pulled up in front of the terminal, he locked the brakes and the car skidded about thirty feet. Maybe he was frustrated with himself that he did not carry out his threat. I exited the taxi, very relieved that I was going home to see my family. Tom jumped out of the taxi, too, and began walking over to me. I thought, *OK, here it comes—he is going to try to sucker punch me as I'm getting my luggage from the trunk.*

So I faced him, in a semi-combative stance. As he got closer to me, I noticed he looked worried rather than antagonistic. He said, in a cracking, halting voice: "Jesse, do you think if I die tonight, I won't go to heaven?" Well, he asked the right guy, because I was not going to give him some politically correct, watered-down, *Kumbaya*-sounding ecumenism. This is a moment described by James: "Let him know that whoever brings back a sinner from the error of his way will save his soul from death and will cover a multitude of sins" (James 5:20).

I told him, "Tom, you spent the last ten minutes blaspheming the holy name of Jesus. You are a baptized Catholic. You must repent, believe, and come back home to Holy Mother Church."

He just looked at me and walked away. He was still seething with anger as he got back into the taxi and sped off.

Where is Tom today? I don't know. I do know this: The Lord gives each of us opportunities to evangelize. I used this particular opportunity to stand up for Jesus and speak "the truth in love" (Ephesians 4:15). Jesus says: "You will know the truth, and the truth will set you free" (John 8:32).

Brothers and sisters, we can take a cue from Prince Hector in the movie *Troy*.[57] He told his soldiers right before the battle against the Greeks: "Trojans, all my life I have lived by a code. And the code is simple: honor the gods, love your women, and defend your country. Troy is mother to us all—fight for her." I say the same to you, fellow Catholic warriors: "All my life I have lived by a code. And the code is simple: Honor God, love your wife, and defend your Church. The

Church is mother to us all—fight for her!"

Pope Benedict XVI said on Easter Sunday 2009: "Let no one draw back from this peaceful battle that has been launched by Christ's Resurrection. Christ is looking for men and women who will help him to affirm his victory using his weapons— the weapons of justice, truth, mercy, forgiveness, and love."[58]

For Reflection

1. Do you wake up with a sense of purpose and mission each day? What is it?
2. What regrets (if any) do you have as you look back over your life? What can you do today to live differently, so that ten years from now, you can look back with no regrets?
3. Have you ever had a life-threatening encounter? If so, how did you respond—with the Holy Spirit's power and courage, or did you let fear rule? What can you do today to live a more courageous Christian life?

CHAPTER SIXTEEN

Your Faith or Your Career

We must obey God rather than man.
—Acts 5:29

Do you stand up for your faith? Have you ever been in a situation where you had to choose between your faith or your career? Here's what happened to me.

I was a rookie deputy sheriff, on my first patrol assignment, which involved working one of the toughest areas of the city. I was proud to wear the badge. I was physically fit, wrote good reports, was an expert shooter, had an optimistic attitude, and was known as a gung-ho cop. I had a good reputation with the veteran officers, the local judge, and the district attorney's office. My career was blossoming.

One particular morning, I attended a briefing before "hitting the streets." The watch commander, Lieutenant Agnostic, briefed the deputies regarding activity in the streets over the last twenty-four hours. He stated that there were some "Jesus Freaks" who were picketing an abortion clinic and intimidating the women seeking "medical treatment." The lieutenant ordered us to disperse these "Jesus freaks," arresting them if we had to. He told us that the abortion clinic doctor donated generously to our Youth Athletic League and Drug Awareness program and was a personal friend of the sheriff.

The deputies were dismissed from the briefing, and I waited around to speak to the lieutenant. The room emptied and it was just me and him. After telling me how highly he thought of me and how I was the paradigm of a rookie deputy sheriff, he asked me what was on my mind. Not knowing how he would react, I mustered up the courage to ask him if I could work the desk or the jail tonight in lieu of working the streets. "Why?" he asked, surprised.

I told him that I was a practicing Catholic who was pro-life. I told him that my parents and many of my church friends have picketed outside of abortion clinics, and I could not in good conscience arrest peaceful pro-life sidewalk counselors.

The lieutenant instantly turned hostile. He told me that I needed to keep my religion at home and not bring it to work. He reminded me that I was a government employee who worked for a paramilitary organization, and he was giving me a direct order to go out and "arrest those [expletive] Jesus freaks."

I asked the lieutenant a second time if he would please honor my request because I had a true moral problem arresting decent Christians who were exercising their constitutional right of free speech. I reminded the lieutenant that the streets were plagued by real criminals, and I felt that this detail was a waste of law enforcement resources and tax dollars.

The lieutenant responded by saying that if I defied his orders, he would write me up and recommend my suspension without pay to the captain. I weighed this threat against the fact that my wife was pregnant with our second child, we had just bought a house with a sizeable mortgage, and we had a brand-new car with a four-year payment plan.

What to Do?

I was in a quandary. I had witnessed police behavior during mass arrests at civil demonstrations. It's a lose-lose situation—both citizens and deputies get hurt, and the city pays for legal and medical bills, which come from our taxes. The first solution would be smooth things out with my lieutenant, go out there, and gain the trust and respect of my coworkers. I could rationalize that I had to comply with orders. I reasoned that:

I didn't want to look like a wimp in front of the rest of my coworkers.

I was under the orders of the lieutenant; he was in command.

I certainly couldn't afford to be suspended without pay based on my present standard of living.

I could stand at a distance and not partake of the actual physical arrest of the pro-lifers. I could turn away so I wouldn't witness any police abuse just in case there was any.

Another part of me, my moral conscience, reminded me that my Catholic faith was something I was supposed to live out privately as well as publicly. I recalled what the bishop told me at my confirmation: "You are a soldier of Christ." I remembered last Sunday's homily, where the priest quoted two verses: "For God did not give us a spirit of timidity but a spirit of power and love and self-control" (2 Timothy 1:7) and "But whoever denies me before men, I also will deny before my Father who is in heaven" (Matthew 10:33).

I thought about the respect my wife and church community had for me, as a catechist, lector, and prayer group leader in my parish. The Miraculous Medal I wore around my neck felt like it was burning, and I was beginning to feel physically nauseous. Should I follow my Catholic moral conscience and get written up for insubordination and put my job in jeopardy?

This lieutenant, a well-respected, decorated Vietnam veteran, had a reputation for handing out discipline and suspensions. He had the power to bounce me around from shift to shift from one week to the next, and he also had the power to change my days off from one week to the next. I suddenly remembered that he would be writing my yearly evaluation in the next couple of days, and he could destroy my career on paper.

I took a deep breath and told the lieutenant, "With all due respect, what you are asking me to do goes against my moral conscience and my faith. I can't do what you are asking me to do."

He answered, "Don't push me. I'd better see you at the abortion clinic in ten minutes—or else."

My Solution

I decided I was going to follow my conscience and not be part of arresting peaceful pro-lifers. This meant defying a direct order from my lieutenant to be part of the arrest team. Instead of following the other patrol cars to the abortion clinic, I drove to an area with several bars. I waited a few minutes until one of the bar's patrons got in his car and began driving, and then I pulled him over, performed a field sobriety test, and arrested him for drunk driving.

The lieutenant called me on the radio and I notified him that I was out of service because I had a prisoner in custody. Impounding the vehicle, booking, fingerprinting, collecting blood from the hospital, and writing the report took about two hours to complete, so I ended up missing the entire arrest detail at the abortion clinic.

While I was still in the station writing up the report, the lieutenant called me into his office and told me, "I know you made that arrest so you could get out of being part of the arrest team at the abortion clinic." He told me he was going to write me up for defying a direct order and suspend me without pay.

I told the lieutenant that I couldn't violate my conscience, and moreover, I stopped to deal with a drunk driver after I left the sheriff's station. The lieutenant saw right through me; he knew that I deliberately arrested this drunk driver exiting a bar in order not to comply with his orders. He knew he wouldn't be able to do anything to me administratively for not assisting at the abortion clinic, since I made a legal arrest en route to the clinic, but he told me he would make my life "hell."

I called my wife after I got chewed out and threatened by the lieutenant, and she came through like a true saint. She told me she supported my decision and thought I did the right thing, she also lifted my spirits by saying she knew Jesus was pleased with my faithfulness. She told me she would pray for me right then, and that no matter what happened, she would stand by me.

Despite all the power the lieutenant had over my career, I had to take a stand and be up front about my religious convictions. If I hadn't, I would live a dual life—like so many Catholics who hide their religious convictions while at work. If I was ridiculed for being a follower of Christ, at least my fellow deputies would know where I draw the line. As the Lord says, "Let what you say be simply 'Yes' or 'No'" (Matthew 5:37).

Was this the best way to handle this situation? It might not have been in the here and now, but in the grand scheme of eternity it was. In the words of Peter, the first pope, "We must obey God rather than men" (Acts 5:29). Christ is my King, and to be an obedient knight is far more meritorious than being an obedient cop. I took strength from the words of St. Paul: "I consider that the sufferings of this present time are not worth comparing with the glory that is to be revealed to us" (Romans 8:18). Yes, I did the right thing!

The Outcome

The lieutenant notified the captain, who in turn called me into his office. He told me to have a seat, closed the door, and asked me if

I had defied the lieutenant's direct orders. I said, "Yes, but I can explain." The captain interrupted and said, "You realize I can suspend you without pay for violating the chain of command, and you realize you just committed an act of insubordination against a superior, don't you?"

I said, "Yes, sir, but please let me explain." The captain cut me off again and said, "Is being pro-life such an important core principle of yours that you would even jeopardize your career?"

I replied, "Captain, underneath this badge and uniform beats the heart of a Catholic Christian, which is my deepest identity."

The captain paused for a few seconds (it seemed like an eternity), stood up, shook my hand and then offered his support for my actions, specifically expressing the wish that more deputies displayed such a sense of their own core principles.

I was speechless. The only thought in my mind was "Thank you, Jesus, I trust in you." The words of the psalmist were a good description of how God brought resolution to this matter: "Sit at my right hand till I make your enemies your footstool" (Psalm 110:1).

For Reflection

1. Have you ever had a situation at work where you were asked to do something that violated your conscience—something you considered unethical? How did you respond?

2. Do you think it was the right decision to defy a lieutenant's orders? Why or why not? Would you have handled the situation differently?

3. Should your Catholic moral conscience affect your behavior at work?

CHAPTER SEVENTEEN

Lessons Learned: The Story of Samson and Delilah

"And the Spirit of the Lord came down
mightily on [Samson.]"
—Judges 14:19

Another colorful and beloved story—particularly for men—is the epic Old Testament tale of Samson, found in Judges 13—16. Samson was a wild beast of a man; it is difficult to understand how he could even be called a man of God. He was a judge of Israel, and yet he had never led an army against the enemy. Instead, in his own brutish way, he antagonized and brutalized the Philistines (who were Israel's enemies) all by himself—He was an "army of one." He was so strong that he killed a lion with his bare hands.

The story of Samson dates back to the days of the judges in Israel (before the ascendancy of the kings). Israel was not yet a unified nation, just a loose group of tribes, constantly being attacked by their enemies. When the people called upon the Lord to deliver them from their distress, he would send them a man or a woman to lead them against their enemies. These individual were the judges.

Samson was part of the tribe of Dan, north of the Gaza Strip. This land was occupied by the Philistines, and the Israelites could not gain a foothold there. Samson was from this area, and he was raised to be one of the leaders. Samson should have been fighting against the Philistine men, but instead he would rather be playing with the Philistine women. Samson was a mighty warrior—he grew up to be a man of tremendous strength, and his parents consecrated him to

God through the Nazarite vow, which meant, in part, that he could not cut his hair (see Judges 13:5). The Nazarites were a group noted for their special dedication to God. The Nazarites symbolized their special dedication by never cutting their hair or partaking in strong drink. Samson's true strength was his covenant and vow with God. His hair was an outward manifestation of that covenant with God. According to the story, Samson's strength lay in the great seven locks of hair that flowed from his head.

So, if Samson ever were to cut his hair, it would mean that his fidelity and strength would be gone. Samson was a big strong guy who demonstrated his devotion to the Lord by his Nazarite vow. But he was also a big joker—I think he must have been fun to be around. He always had a trick up his sleeve. The story of Samson illustrates both his sense of loyalty to God and his human weakness jeopardized his strength. In the end, his strength became his weakness.

Chapter 16 relates how he began to be a womanizer. "Samson… saw a harlot, and he went into her" (v.1). Samson fell hard for the harlot Delilah—she must have been very beautiful. The Philistines were crafty. They knew his weakness for women, so they had Delilah seduce him in order to see where his strength came from. It's interesting to note that the name *Samson* means "Sunshine," and the name *Delilah* means "Night" or "Darkness." In this story we see the darkness of the Philistines eclipse the sunshine of the Israelites.

Samson was in the wrong country looking at the wrong things. He had no business checking out the Philistine women who worshiped false gods or thinking about marrying one of them. He was now in a place where he shouldn't be and considering things he should have been avoiding altogether. Does this sound like anyone you know? In the Act of Contrition, we promise to avoid near occasions of sin. We should develop the habit of asking ourselves why we are in certain places. What are we doing there?

Samson didn't engage in this level of self-examination, however. Instead he began to toy around with sin. This provided Delilah with the opportunity to engage him in conversation in order to discover the source of his strength. Samson was like Esau, selling his birthright— not for some pottage, but for sexual pleasure. Samson's passion caused him to stop valuing the things of God. He was guilty of presumption; he thought he could sin with impunity and still have God's protection and friendship. Delilah was persistent and seductive, and she eventually got Samson to tell her the truth. Samson gave up his unique relationship with God for sexual pleasure. What's even worse, he doesn't even realize it was gone! Judges 13:20 says, "He did not know that the Lord had left him."

Samson was living in a very dangerous place. Instead of living by faith, he was living by sight. Samson saw what he wanted, he lusted after it, he coveted it, and he took it. He was living for the sole purpose of fulfilling the pleasures of the flesh. He was trying to satisfy the "here and now." God gave Samson free will, just as he has given it to every one of us. Samson had the ability to make choices. Samson did not want what his parents had, nor did he want to submit to their authority. He did not want what God wanted for him, either. His mind was set on what he wanted to do, and he was deceived by his own selfishness and pride. Samson knew that God had called him; he knew he had been gifted with tremendous strength. He thought that having these special abilities gave him a license to live any way he wanted. Because God in his patience did not deal with him immediately, Samson assumed that it was okay to follow his disordered passions. He misinterpreted his own free will as God's permissiveness.

It often begins with one little compromise, but then, before you know it, you are entangled so deeply in sin that you can't get free. It ended up destroying Samson. Though he had taken a Nazarite vow to live a separate and holy life before God, he ended up compromising his belief and values as he grew older. Driven by his lust, Samson visited places he was not supposed to visit, ate foods he was forbidden to eat, and mingled with people he shouldn't have mingled with. He spent days and even years allowing himself to be seduced by Philistine women. His vow of separation from the world and dedication to the Lord was long forgotten as he sought one pretty face after another, finally marrying Delilah.

Samson's Demise

Delilah finally coaxed Samson into telling her the source of his strength—the fact that his hair had never been cut. Once Delilah knew the secret of Samson's great strength, she waited until he was asleep and had another man shave off Samson's seven locks. Due to Delilah's craftiness, the Philistines were able to capture and torture him, gouging out his eyes and making him do hard labor. Now Samson was blind, weak, and humiliated, forced to plow the fields like an ox.

The Philistines held a feast, and they decided to amuse themselves at Samson's expense. They brought him to their temple to make fun of him. When he arrived there, he asked to be placed near the central pillars of the building. Then Samson called upon God, asking him to strengthen him one more time so he might destroy the Philistines.

God granted him this favor, but Samson still had to make reparation for his sins by paying the ultimate sacrifice and giving up his own life in the act of God's justice upon the unbelieving Philistines. Samson pulled down the pillars, causing the temple to collapse on him and all the Philistines. He died as he had lived—violent but contrite and rededicated to the Lord. As they say, it's not how slow you start the race, but how strong you finish. Samson started his faith walk slow but ended strong.

Samson eventually reaped what he sowed, and so will each one of us. Have you crossed the line? Have you compromised and played with sin? Turn to Christ now. Get back to Mass, the sacraments, the rosary, fellowship, daily Bible reading, and prayer. As you walk daily with the Lord, you will receive God's strength to resist the power of sin and compromise in your life.

The story of Samson and Delilah has caught the imagination of poets, artists, and filmmakers. It teaches us the lesson that even the most powerful among us can fall victim to temptation. The loss of Samson's hair signified the loss of something much more important—the loss of his relationship with God. The return of Samson's hair along with his power accompanies his repentance and the renewal of his faith. His destruction of the temple of Dagon, along with hundreds of Philistines, symbolizes Gods power, a power that can crush the false gods of Canaan—and the false gods of this present darkness.

For Reflection

1. What temptations in your own life have threatened to derail your relationship with God?

2. How conscious are you on a daily basis of God's presence in your life?

3. What can you do to strengthen your intimacy with God so you can increase his power in your life?

CHAPTER EIGHTEEN

Humility: A Powerful Weapon

Walk in a manner worthy of the calling to which you have
been called, with all lowliness and meekness, with patience,
forbearing one another in love, eager to maintain the unity
of the Spirit in the bond of peace.
—Ephesians 4:1–2

I am a retired cop, a retired amateur boxer and kick boxer, and a certi-
fied wrestling coach. My two boys are wrestlers. My oldest son, Paul,
is a soldier in the Army Reserves and a Jiu-Jitsu practitioner. Needless
to say, there is a lot of testosterone in the Romero household.

In fact, many of my friends are somewhat intrigued with my background, and they have asked me if I have recorded any of my fights.
In fact I have them posted on YouTube. If you type in "Jesse Romero's
fight montage," you can watch 7:11 seconds of the young, aggressive, intense, combative Jesse Romero. At the end of the video, it
says, "Jesse now preaches the Catholic gospel with the same fero-
cious spirit."

I believe that I am the only Catholic evangelist in the world that
carries a Bible in one hand, a rosary in my pocket, and a gun on my
hip. (As a retired deputy sheriff, I have a concealed carry weapon
permit in all fifty states.)

Why do I disclose all of the above "man credentials"? I'm sure some
of you might have the impression that I am hard, unbending, and
aggressive in everything I do. Not true! There is a deeply emotional
side to me that has grown as my love for Our Lord Jesus Christ has

grown. The *Catechism* calls this *interior conversion* (see *CCC*, 1428, 1430). Paragraph 1432 says:

> The human heart is heavy and hardened. God must give man a new heart. Conversion is first of all a work of the grace of God who makes our hearts return to him: "Restore us to thyself, O LORD, that we may be restored!" God gives us the strength to begin anew. It is in discovering the greatness of God's love that our heart is shaken by the horror and weight of sin and begins to fear offending God by sin and being separated from him. The human heart is converted by looking upon him whom our sins have pierced: Let us fix our eyes on Christ's blood and understand how precious it is to his Father, for, poured out for our salvation it has brought to the whole world the grace of repentance.

A Lesson in Humility

Back in 2004, I gave a series of weekly lectures at the Catholic Resource Center in West Covina, California. I covered the following topics in my apologetics class: justification by faith alone, Marian dogmas, the biblical roots of the papacy, the Eucharist, *Sola Scriptura*, and eternal salvation. This class was packed wall-to-wall with students. I noticed a young Hispanic male in his early thirties wearing a suit and tie and carrying a Protestant study Bible and a Greek interlinear Bible. When I started off with the opening prayer, I could tell he was not Catholic because he did not make the Sign of the Cross. One of my students told me, "Jesse, that guy is a pastor—he opened up an evangelical church a couple of miles from here."

I immediately sensed he was there to see if there was any biblical basis for Catholic teachings. He appeared to be open-minded, and he flipped his Bible from one page to another every time I shared a verse of Scripture. He listened intently as I explained the Scripture in light of Catholic hermeneutics (relying on the Fathers of the Church, saints, popes, and papal councils). At the end of the first night of class, he came up to me and introduced himself. He told me that he was a newly ordained evangelical pastor; he had graduated from BIOLA University (Bible Institute of Los Angeles) with a double master's degree, one in sacred Scripture and a minor in Koine Greek.

He said, "Objectively speaking, it looks like you Catholics are correct on the doctrine of justification." I asked him to come back the following week so we could continue our dialogue in charity as brothers in Christ. He promised that he would come again.

The following week I taught on Mary in the Bible. He had the same reaction, admitting that the Catholic biblical arguments were compelling and convincing, and that he had never seen these verses of Scripture explained this way before. When I taught on the papacy, he had the same reaction. He basically said, "Looks like you Catholics are right again."

The next week I taught on the Real Presence of Jesus Christ in the Holy Eucharist, and he had the same positive reaction. He conceded that the Catholic position is in line with Scripture, and in my heart I was saying, "Yes, Lord, yes!"

It was the same when I taught on the issue of *sola Scriptura* (the Bible alone as the sole rule of faith). Again he conceded that the Catholic position based on Scripture, common sense, history, and the Fathers of the Church was overwhelming.

The final week of this lecture series I taught on eternal security— Can a Christian Lose His or Her Salvation? This young pastor was present, following my every word and nodding his head up and down in agreement. When I finished the lecture, he came up to me and we exchanged pleasantries. He told me that he was intellectually stimulated and deeply impressed with my knowledge of Sacred Scripture, History and Apologetics. He confessed that if he had met me years before, he probably would not have gone to BIOLA. He admitted that he was struck like lightning with biblical and historical truth, which was not at all what he expected by attending my class.

Finally I asked him rather sheepishly, "Well then, what is keeping you from becoming a Catholic Christian?" He then revealed that he had been born and raised Catholic but had been deeply wounded by the Church when he was younger. He told me that a teacher had scolded, berated, and demeaned him in confirmation class in front of the entire class. I just listened to him, becoming his sounding board as his voice got louder and angrier.

We walked out to the parking lot; by that time our two cars were the only ones left in the parking lot. I told him that painful things happened because the Church is made up of human beings. We may hold the Church to a higher ideal, but the reality is that the Church is made up of broken vessels and people make mistakes. I said one more time, "You should consider coming back to the Church."

Again, he became defensive, and suddenly I thought, *I need to humble myself and ask for his forgiveness on my knees.* My next thought was, *I'm not going to get on my knees for any one. In fact, no man has ever been able to knock me off of my feet in more than sixty fights in the ring, and no criminal in the streets of Los Angeles County ever took me off of my feet when I was a cop.*

But then I told myself that if I loved God and his Church, I would throw myself at his feet and ask him for forgiveness. Reflexively I fell on my knees in front of him. I clasped his hands in mine, and I told him to find it in his heart to forgive the Catholic Church in Jesus's name. For a second I thought about how this scene would look to a passerby, but then I thought, *Who cares? I'll be a "fool for Christ"* [see 1 Corinthians 4:10]; *this soul is worth saving and bringing back to holy Mother Church.* If St. John Paul II could forgive a Muslim terrorist who shot him five times in the chest, I could surely humble myself before this wounded soul who had been hurt by a member of my Church.

He sensed the sincerity of my actions; his eyes became teary and he helped me to my feet and we embraced. He said, "Thank you! That's all I've been waiting to hear for the last fifteen years—somebody to apologize to me and invite me back." We hugged each other, and I could feel the pain he was carrying leaving his body and soul. We said good-bye and went our separate ways.

I thought about him every day, and I lifted him up in prayer. I saw him about a month later at the Long Beach Catholic Family Conference as I walked onto the stage to give my talk. There he was in the front row with a big smile and a St. Benedict medal around his neck. He waved at me and yelled, "Jesse, I'm back home!" What an adrenaline rush I felt! I knew that my apologetics arguments only went so far; it was humbling myself in front of him that opened his heart and gave him the grace to forgive the Church and come back home to Rome.

Another Humble Apology

At the height of the clergy sexual scandals in 2002, my pastor, Fr. Steven Guitron, was asked to read a letter from the Cardinal of Los Angeles to the congregation. I asked him if I could make a brief pulpit announcement before the final benediction. I told him that I wanted to invite anyone who had been hurt by the Church to meet me out in the courtyard after Mass. Basically I said, "If anybody here today has been hurt by the Church, please meet me outside after Mass so I can personally get on my knees and apologize to you." After Mass, I went to the courtyard and about fifteen people joined me. I prayed, "Lord, your body, blood, soul, and divinity are in me now, so please give me the grace to humble myself." Trust me when I say humility does not come easy for me (just ask my wife).

I took every parishioner in line by the hand, looked into his or her eyes, and asked that person to briefly tell me his or her story. I listened attentively, then got down on my knees and said, "Please find it in your heart to forgive our Church; please forgive her, and I am so glad you are here today." At least a third of them said, "All I ever wanted was an apology from the Church." I hugged each one of them. I don't think these actions make me any less of a man—in fact, I believe these actions helped me grow in virtue. One definition of *virtue* in Merriam-Webster's dictionary is "manly strength or courage." God doesn't answer email; he answers knee-mail.

The fact that the Catholic Church has survived for two thousand years demonstrates that the Holy Spirit has kept her alive and growing despite its sinful members. On March 12, 2000, Pope John Paul II publicly apologized for past and present sins committed by Catholics in the name of the Church:

> Let us pray that each one of us, looking to the Lord Jesus, meek and humble of heart, will recognize that even men of the Church, in the name of faith and morals, have sometimes used methods not in keeping with the Gospel in the solemn duty of defending the truth.
>
> Lord, God of all men and women, in certain periods of history Christians have at times given in to intolerance and

have not been faithful to the great commandment of love, sullying in this way the face of the Church, your Spouse. Have mercy on your sinful children and accept our resolve to seek and promote truth in the gentleness of charity, in the firm knowledge that truth can prevail only in virtue of truth itself. We ask this through Christ our Lord. Amen.[59]

St Paul assures us "that in everything God works for good with those who love him" (Romans 8:28). When someone is hurt by the Church, it is difficult to imagine how anything good could come from it. It is only by following the path of forgiveness that the pain eventually subsides and a deep peace embraces the soul. This is the essence of spiritual healing. The "peace of God, which passes all understanding" (Philippians 4:7) is a peace the world cannot give.

I'm Staying

Often people tell me, "Jesse, I'm seriously considering leaving the faith. My pastor and others at my parish do not live up to what they are teaching. How can the Church be true when it produces such hypocrisy?" I like to tell them the following story:

Once there was a young priest who was asked by his bishop to go to a certain parish and help a certain older priest. This older priest embezzled funds from the parish, had a mistress, and was an alcoholic. The young priest did his best to help the older priest by setting a good example for him, but nothing he did seemed to work. Discouraged, the young priest finally gave up and packed his bags. Before he left, he made one last visit to the Tabernacle. He said, "I'm sorry Lord. I failed, and now I'm leaving." The young priest turned away and walked down the long aisle. Suddenly, from the altar, he heard Christ's voice, saying simply, "I'm staying." No matter how many corrupt clergy there are, I'm staying. No matter how many lukewarm Catholics there are, I'm staying. No matter how many leave the Church, I'm staying.

For Reflection

1. Have you ever felt (or do you sometimes feel) like leaving the Catholic Church? If so, why? And if you actually did leave the Church and then return, what motivated you to do so?

2. How do you explain the atrocities done by the clergy to someone who is outside the Church looking in?

3. Have you, or someone close to you, ever been hurt by someone in authority you trusted? Have you been able to forgive that person?

CHAPTER NINETEEN

Ongoing Conversion–Renew Your Mind

Do not be conformed to this world but be transformed by
the renewal of your mind, that you may prove what is the will
of God, what is good and acceptable and perfect.
—Romans 12:2

Each of us has two purposes in life: general and specific. Your general purpose in life is to be holy and get to heaven. Your specific purpose in life is your vocation—your state in life. Too many believers miss this high calling, failing to ever grow past the infant stage in their faith.

Once you are born again through the sacrament of baptism absolutely nothing will change in your life unless you begin the process of *renewing your mind*—changing the way your mind operates.

This is because your flesh is still being controlled by your mind. Your body does what your mind tells it to do. Renewing your mind is another way of saying changing your mindset, and it is this new mindset that allows a Catholic believer to develop brand-new godly attitudes, goals, ideals, opinions, desires, appetites and ideas.

Unfortunately for most Catholic Christians, their spiritual growth stops after they receive the sacrament of confirmation; they stop learning about their faith and don't think much about the way they think. But I am here to tell you that when you receive the sacrament of confirmation, it's just the beginning. Confirmation empowers and compels you to live as a disciple of Christ.

The Holy Spirit is there to help you, but he can only assist you if do your part. The Lord will never force his love and will on you. That is why so many Catholics continue to commit the same old sins and have the same old shortcomings, never making much progress in their spiritual lives.

Just because you are born again through baptism and born of the Spirit through confirmation, that doesn't mean that God is suddenly going to show up and magically change you into a holy, happy saint. After confirmation you'll still have to deal with disordered appetites, such as a bad temper if another person "gets in your face" or cuts you off in traffic. You're still going to succumb to the lure of alcohol, drugs, or other mind-altering substances. You'll still be tempted to watch those questionable programs on television. You'll still wrestle with concupiscence—the inclination toward evil and sin. As the *Catechism* says:

> As a result of original sin, human nature is weakened in its powers, subject to ignorance, suffering, and the domination of death, and inclined to sin (this inclination is called "concupiscence"). (*CCC* 418)

The sad truth is that many Catholics still live in misery. They are still enslaved to sins that make them miserable, depressed, or even suicidal. They still curse people out, bully the weak, and drink too much.

Confirmation is a powerful sacrament. Whether you remember it or not, when you received the sacrament of confirmation, God gave you the grace to be a soldier of Christ (2 Timothy 1:6–7; 2:3–4). You told God that you really and truly wanted to turn your life around. When you received the gift of the Holy Spirit, you made a decision to no longer follow the ways of the world, but from that point on you intended to follow Jesus Christ. God gave you a new heart when you were baptized (see Ezekiel 36:25–27), but experiencing that new heart requires *changing the way you think* about your life.

The Key to Victorious Living

The key to living triumphantly as a Christian is combining your new heart with a renewed mind. Prayer, regular confession, and frequent reception of Holy Communion keep your mind renewed. If you follow this road map, you will experience amazing transformations in your life. This is the meaning of conversion; this is the process of surrendering your entire life to Jesus Christ every day, in both good times and bad.

If you think about it, you can't really start on your road to spiritual growth and spiritual maturity without a whole new mindset. Remember that your mind controls every single one of your actions. Your mind controls your thoughts. Your mind tells your body what to do. You speak what's on your mind. Your mind tells your eyes what to look at and your ears what things to pay attention to and what things to tune out. Your mind is integral to the way you respond in every single situation.

Even as a Christian, the secular world, the flesh, and the devil will continue to greatly influence you. But if you are willing to follow Jesus Christ and put your Catholic faith into daily, minute-by-minute practice, you will begin to look at everything differently. The battle being waged by Satan against you is designed to take control of your mind, because if Satan can control your mind, he can influence your heart. Your marching orders are to renew your mind through prayer, a life of virtue, and practicing your Catholic faith.

We have to make a conscious effort to surrender our entire life to Jesus Christ. That means giving Jesus complete control over your body, heart, soul, and mind. In order to do this, you must stay in contact with Jesus Christ twenty-four hours a day, seven days a week. You should run everything by Jesus. In other words, if you have a desire to have a few drinks, first talk to Jesus about it. When you are deciding what to watch on TV, ask Jesus his opinion. When you're choosing which friends to hang out with, don't forget to ask Jesus what he thinks about it. He will definitely answer you. He will impress his answers on your heart and mind. He will speak to your conscience. He will influence your character. He will help you to become the best version of yourself.

Eventually you will develop spiritual self-mastery, and this will allow you to overcome sin. Take every thought to Jesus. Do the same thing with each sin—take it to Jesus, bad memories, depressing feelings, and all—and ask Jesus to heal them. The devil wants to take your mind off God. He wants you to struggle with your problems on your own, apart from Jesus—he knows that Jesus is your strength. This is what I mean when I say that hard work and effort are required to renew your mind.

Never forget, though, the Holy Spirit is within you, ready and willing to assist you. When you keep the lines of communication open through prayerful conversation with Christ all day long, you are "practicing the presence of God"—you are living in the power of the Holy Spirit. Constantly listen for God's still, small voice to speak to your heart, mind, and conscience. Here are a few verses to commit to memory:

> I always take pains to have a clear conscience toward God and toward men. (Acts 24:16)

> The aim of our charge is love that issues from a pure heart and a good conscience and sincere faith.... This charge I commit

to you…that you may wage the good warfare, holding faith and a good conscience. By rejecting conscience, certain persons have made shipwreck of their faith. (1 Timothy 1:5, 18–19)

Baptism…now saves you, not as a removal of dirt from the body but as an appeal to God for a clear conscience, through the resurrection of Jesus Christ. (1 Peter 3:21)

Not a One-Time Event

And when you do sin, talk to Jesus about it immediately—go to confession as soon as possible. Ask the Lord to help you analyze why you committed that sin, what circumstances cause you to sin, and what steps you can take to prevent any future occurrence of that sin. You can go through this process every time you sin. And you'll have to do it over and over.

As you can see, renewing your mind is not a one-time event—it's a lifelong process. It's a lifestyle. Renewing your mind only makes sense if you sincerely want to live a godly life. Renewing the mind is only for the believer who truly wants to surrender his or her life fully over to Jesus Christ.

Renewing the mind is not for the part-time Christian or for those who obey God only when it suits them. Renewing the mind is a waste of time for such people because there is no hunger or thirst for Jesus Christ in their hearts. Jesus Christ is not at the center of their lives.

You can renew your mind by staying in a constant state of prayerful communication with Jesus Christ. You cannot take your eyes off of him for a second—not in this world. Not when sin is pressing in on you from every conceivable angle. But if you constantly and continuously keep your focus on Jesus Christ, for the most part sin will be eradicated from your life.

The Three Cs of the Christian Warrior

God is not picking on you; he is making you holy. Sometimes struggles are exactly what we need in our lives. If God allowed us to go through our lives without any obstacles, it would cripple us. We would not be as strong as what we could have been. The Christian is no stranger to danger or suffering.

As Christians we need to set our face like flint against the world, feel the fire in our faces, and be unafraid—because our God is a mighty King. Being a Christian is a *choice*; it's a *challenge*; and it requires *change*! If you were accused and arrested for being a Christian, would there be sufficient evidence to convict you?

Being a Christian warrior also involves *conditioning* (good works); *concentration* (prayer); *and coachability* (obedience). To live like a Christian, you must practice being one. No pain, no gain; no guts, no glory. Christians never take the easy way out; they pay the price. Victory belongs to the persevering.

Your mind—how you think—is crucial to your faith in Jesus Christ. A good way to renew your mind is to meditate often on the following Scriptures:

> Rejoice in the Lord always; again I will say, Rejoice. Let all men know your forbearance. The Lord is at hand. Have no anxiety about anything, but in everything by prayer and supplication with thanksgiving let your requests be made known to God. And the peace of God, which passes all understanding, will keep your hearts and your minds in Christ Jesus. Finally, brethren, whatever is true, whatever is honorable, whatever is just, whatever is pure, whatever is lovely, whatever is gracious, if there is any excellence, if there is anything worthy of praise, think about these things. What

you have learned and received and heard and seen in me, do; and the God of peace will be with you. (Philippians 4:4–9)

Love is patient and kind; love is not jealous or boastful; it is not arrogant or rude. Love does not insist on its own way; it is not irritable or resentful; it does not rejoice at wrong, but rejoices in the right. Love bears all things, believes all things, hopes all things, endures all things. (1 Corinthians 13:4–7)

We destroy arguments and every proud obstacle to the knowledge of God, and take every thought captive to obey Christ. (2 Corinthians 10:5)

Thought is the rudder of life. As William James once said:

Sow a thought—reap an action.
Sow an action—reap a habit.
Sow a habit—reap a character.
Sow a character—reap a destiny.[60]

I don't know about you, but I am too blessed to be stressed! The shortest distance between a problem and a solution is the distance between your knees and the floor. The one who kneels before the Lord can stand up to anything!

For Reflection
1. What specific ways have you found to renew your mind?
2. What happens to your thoughts if you neglect prayer or the sacraments?
3. What does it mean to take every thought captive to Christ?

CHAPTER TWENTY

The Church Militant: Prepare for Glory

Blessed be the Lord my Rock,
who trains my hands for war,
and my fingers for battle.
—Psalm 144:1

The master sword makers of ancient times perfected the art of forging the ideal blade for battle. The different elements were brought together in fire, melted down, and then blended together. Again the metal was heated in the fire, allowing the sword maker to fold it upon itself. It would then be hammered flat and, through the pressure of the pounding, the folded layers adhered to each other. This process was repeated many times, thereby creating dozens and dozens of layers in the blade. The end result was a weapon that was strong enough to keep a sharp edge for battle yet remain flexible enough not to break in the midst of the fight.

This is exactly what we Catholic warriors are meant to be. God is always trying to forge us, sometimes under very intense conditions, so he can build us into strong, disciplined spiritual warriors. That warrior is a man or woman who has the ability to stand up at a moment's notice and courageously defend what is honorable, and do it with deep conviction. At the same time, the spiritual warrior is able to master his or her passions and lead with a strong, gentle spirit. Let's stay battle-ready and know that the Spirit of God is the master sword smith.

Observe the Battlefield

There are many reasons why more Catholic Christians don't stand up and fight for the truth. Distraction, insecurity, selfishness, or being tied down by some habitual sin are just a few of those reasons. Another reason some don't stand in the gap and fight is ignorance. Many of our brothers and sisters in Christ are "low-information Catholics." These are Catholics with a lack of knowledge about the basics of the faith. And it can seem easier to stay in the dark regarding the intentions and attacks of those who want to destroy what is of God. Choosing to remain ignorant is an age-old problem. There seems to be a little voice inside our heads that, if we let it, will convince us that things aren't really that bad—even though in reality they can be much worse. The more we know about those who are trying to destroy what is holy and noble and the more we understand their tactics, the better chance we have of engaging successfully in the fight. I realize that it can be difficult to think about the different attacks going on in our world. It can feel like too much at times. That is why it is imperative that we study and remember the word of God. "Have I not commanded you? Be strong and courageous. Do not be afraid; do not be discouraged, for the Lord your God will be with you wherever you go" (Joshua 1:9). We must be ready for the battle, because whether we ignore it or not, the fight is upon us.

Each of us must act upon a higher level of commitment and involvement. We need to call each other to arms as well. Here are some ways to ready yourself for the battle:

1. Increase your prayer and fasting, a little at a time.
2. Stay close to God through frequent reception of the sacraments.
3. Increase your Scripture reading.

4. Be vocal in defending and spreading the truth, according to your state in life.

5. Don't make excuses for not doing any of these things.

I don't think we realize just how much our families are counting on us. Think about all the souls that you come in contact with every day. Think about the lives you have never met yet—and those you never will meet—in this life. Fight for them all! Souls are at stake! Let's be ready for battle by toughening up! There's too much at stake to be lazy and soft.

Christ demands zeal from his followers. There is nothing anywhere in the gospels that even remotely implies that Jesus is okay with us being lukewarm or mediocre with living our faith. In fact it's pretty clear the exact opposite is the case.

> "I came to cast fire upon the earth; and would that it were already kindled!" (Luke 12:49)

> "Because you are lukewarm, and neither cold nor hot, I will spew you out of my mouth." (Revelation 3:16)

> "He answered, 'You shall love the Lord your God with all your heart, and with all your soul, and with all your strength, and with all your mind; and your neighbor as yourself.'" (Luke 10:27)

These are just a few statements about zeal found in the New Testament; there are many more. We each have free will. We each have the ability to make the choice whether or not we are going to let the ways of this world water us down. It can be easy to allow the concerns of this life to throw water on the fire that Christ wants ignited in our souls. It is very easy to give into the temptation of being lazy and dull when it comes to keeping ourselves sharp.

Are you maintaining the temple of the Holy Spirit with regular exercise and healthy eating habits? As a soldier of Christ, you have the duty to keep yourself sharp: body, mind, and soul. If you have been charged with the care of others, you have the duty to be sharp for them as well. You cannot lead others to the glory of heaven if you have little or no understanding of what that means. Without the grace of God, it is impossible to fulfill one's duty. Go to the source. Cooperate with the grace of God. Do what you were put here on earth to do! Get ready for battle, because Christ demands zeal and others are counting on that zeal from you.

Heroes and Heroines

Most men dream doing something heroic at some point in their lives. A man sees himself flying into some intense situation in some dramatic way, where he beats up the bad guy and disables the bomb with three seconds to spare, right before it blows up half the hemisphere.

A lot of guys live out the hero dream by watching the latest greatest action hero defeat villains and save the world. Still other guys step into cyberspace or the world of gaming, and there they conquer, crush, and dominate the bad guys—and then, of course, they save the world.

For some men this hero dream was part of their childhood, but now that they're adults they see themselves as having moved past that so-called childish phase. Maybe this describes you. Maybe you've become so sophisticated or intellectual and mature that the idea of saving the world just doesn't flip your switch. Or maybe you're so distracted or anxious about life in general that the hero dream has been buried under a pile of worry or insecurity, and you're no longer able to see it clearly.

The truth is, both men and women are meant to live heroically. God cut his people from hero cloth. You may never stop a bad guy or disable a bomb three seconds before it explodes, but if you are a husband and father or a priest, if you are a wife and mother, then you are the hero or heroine in the eyes of those God has given you to care for. You are the hero or heroine of their worlds.

The souls entrusted to you observe you—they see how you take on the attacks of the world, the flesh, and the devil. They watch how you deal with your own weaknesses and what you do to rise above your failings to defeat evil, especially the sin within your own heart.

Go to the source of heroic strength daily: Jesus Christ in his Word and in the Eucharist. Get ready to do battle, because heroes need to stay sharp and alert. Souls are counting on you. Trust God. Pray the rosary. This is a great time to be a Catholic Christian! We know that we are on the winning side. God is not dead—he's not even tired.

Remember, a true hero keeps fighting even when he doesn't hear any epic music. We are so used to seeing the heroes in movies save the day in dramatic fashion, complete with talented actors, special effects, and a grand music score. It gives us a rush. I understand that—I enjoy a good movie told with excitement and drama. Life itself is full of drama. God has wired us to relate to these movies loaded with action.

Can you have a better storyteller than Christ himself? The dynamics of his presentation is flawless. Most importantly, though, is the teaching and hope Jesus pours out for us. There was no musical score playing that day when he was put to death on the cross that devastatingly Good Friday. No special effects. But the explosions and pyrotechnics of the spiritual realm were off the charts. Death was being defeated! The spiritual war was being fully fought. Our world has a difficult time connecting with this. The greatest heroic moments that are truly rooted in the imitation of Christ are oftentimes unseen and underappreciated. Calvary didn't look like a glorious victory.

But the true Catholic hero moves forward regardless. He is not dismayed or frightened by the villain or his thuggish, diabolical attacks, no matter how small or large they may be. Remember, too, that in heaven the epic music is perfect—and it never ends! We must live battle-ready because we are all created to be heroes and heroines in Christ.

In the end we have the certainty that truth will triumph over lies, light over darkness, and good over evil. So stand firm, Catholic warriors, and rush to the battle lines with Jesus in your heart, a rosary in one hand and a Bible in the other. No matter what happens during this earthly battle, we know that Christ the King wins the war. Jesus Christ heals, Jesus Christ saves, and Jesus Christ sets us free. Jesus Christ came to save the lost, the last, and the least. *Viva Cristo Rey* (Long Live Christ the King)—Christ is our hope!

For Reflection

1. How deep is the level of your commitment to Christ? How can you increase it?
2. Do you see your body as the temple of the Holy Spirit? What would you do differently if you truly saw yourself this way?
3. What kinds of heroism are you called to in your own family? At work? In your community?

1. Fulton Sheen, Foreword to *Radio Replies* Vol. 1 (St. Paul, Minn.: Radio Replies Press Society, 1938), p. ix.
2. Message of the Holy Father John Paul II to the Youth of the World on the Occasion of the IV World Youth Day, August 1989, http://www.vatican.va/holy_father/john_paul_ii/messages/youth/documents/hf_jp-ii_mes_27111988_iv-world-youth-day_en.html.
3. Adapted from "The Fellowship of the Unashamed," http://home.snu.edu/~hculbert/commit.htm.
4. Cardinal Wuerl, " 'Tsunami of Secularism' Has Swept the Cultural Landscape," http://www.ewtn.com/vnews/getstory.asp?number=121728.

Chapter Three

5. Dinesh D'Souza, *What's So Great About Christianity?* (Carol Stream, Ill.: Tyndale, 2008).
6. D'Souza, pp. 197–198.
7. D'Souza, pp. 198–199.
8. Pascal Lectures, University of Waterloo. http://home.apu.edu/~jsimons/Bio101/quotes5.htm.
9. Robert Jastrow - astronomer, physicist and cosmologist; Have astronomers found God? 1980, *Reader's Digest,* v. 117 (699), pp. 49–53.
10. D'Souza, p. 214.
11. Henri de Lubac, *The Drama of Atheist Humanism (San Francisco: Ignatius, 1995).*

Chapter Five

12. *Magnificat,* August 17, 2012.

Chapter Six

13. Patrick A. Trueman, "The Pornography Pandemic," http://www.kofc.org/en/columbia/detail/2011_11_computer.html.

14. Jack Wintz, O.F.M., "Anima Christi: A Mystical Prayer," http://www.americancatholic.org/e-news/friarjack/Newlayout.aspx?id=105.

15. Quoted at Amy Welborn, "Suscipe, the Radical Prayer," http://www.ignatianspirituality.com/ignatian-prayer/prayers-by-st-ignatius-and-others/suscipe-the-radical-prayer/.

16. "Consecration to Mary," http://www.catholic.org/prayers/prayer.php?p=441.

Chapter Seven

17. Dave Grossman, "On Sheep, Wolves, and Sheepdogs," http://www.gleamingedge.com/mirrors/onsheepwolvesandsheepdogs.html.

18. Adapted from "10 Ways to Wait for Sex until Marriage," by Pregnancy Counseling Center, Mission Hills, California, www.PCCofSFV.com.

19. http://www.merriam-webster.com/dictionary/coward.

20. The original "Soldier's Creed" is available at http://www.army.mil/values/soldiers.html.

Chapter Eight

21. "1992 Los Angeles Riots," http://www.docstoc.com/docs/6462958/1992_Los_Angeles_Riots.

22. "1992 Los Angeles Riots," http://www.docstoc.com/docs/6462958/1992_Los_Angeles_Riots.

23. "1992 Los Angeles Riots," http://www.docstoc.com/docs/6462958/1992_Los_Angeles_Riots.

24. http://en.wikipedia.org/wiki/1992_Los_Angeles_riots.

25. "The Driver's Prayer," http://www.catholictradition.org/Two-Hearts/drivers-prayer.htm.

26. St. Alphonsus de Liguori, "The Holy Name of Mary—The Power of Her Name," http://www.themostholyrosary.com/appendix8. htm.

27. "The 15 Promises," http://www.theholyrosary.org/rosarybenefits.

28. St. Louis De Montfort, *The Secret of the Rosary (Rockford, Ill.: TAN, 1987) p. 74.*

29. John Paul II, Eucharistic Congress, Philadelphia, August 13, 1976.

30. Adapted from http://tugandregina.blogspot.com/2008/05/rosary-creed.html.

31. St. Louis De Montfort, *The Secret of the Rosary (Rockford, Ill.: TAN, 1987), pp. 148, 144–145.*

Chapter Nine

32. *Diary of St. Faustina (Stockbridge, Mass.: Marian Press, 2010), 1488.*

33. "Act of Hope," http://www.catholic.org/prayers/prayer.php?p=429.

34. Pope John Paul II, *Message for the Proceedings of the World Congress of the Ecclesial Movements*, 2. http://www.vatican. va/roman_curia/pontifical_councils/migrants/documents/ rc_pc_migrants_doc_2003037_renewal_hamao_en.html#_ftn18.

35. Quoted at The Fatima Network, http://www.fatimacrusader.com/ cr18/cr18pgS14a.asp.

36. Holy Father's Speech for the World Congress of Ecclesial Movements and New Communities, http://www.vatican. va/roman_curia/pontifical_councils/laity/documents/ rc_pc_laity_doc_27051998_movements-speech-hf_en.html.

37. Billy Graham, "The Answer to Worry," *Unto the Hills: A Daily Devotional (Nashville: Thomas Nelson, 2010), reading for February 26.*

38. "Particular Examen on the Theological Virtue of Hope," by Father John A. Hardon S.J., http://www.ewtn.com/library/spirit/exam-cons.txt.

Chapter Eleven

39. Walter Martin, *Essential Christianity* (Ventura, Calif.: Regal, 1980), pp. 1, 63.

40. Josh McDowell, *Evidence That Demands a Verdict* (Arrowhead Springs, Calif.: Campus Crusade for Christ, 1975), p. 185. Emphasis in original.

41. Epistle of Ignatius to the Trallians, 10, http://www.pseudepig-rapha.com/LostBooks/ignatius2trallians.htm.

42. William A. Jurgens *The Faith of the Early Fathers, Volume 1 (Collegeville, Minn.: Liturgical, 1970), pp. 101–102.*

43. "The Creed of Tertullian," Catholic Apologetics, http://www.theworkofgod.org/Library/Apologtc/R_Haddad/Ibelieve/creed7.htm.

44. http://www.newadvent.org/fathers/3801.htm.

45. Alexander of Alexandria, *Encyclical Letter to All Non-Egyptian Bishops, 12; http://www.reocities.com/kjkhemraj/Website/Mary_the_Mother_of_God.pdf.*

46. Frank Morrison, *Who Moved the Stone? (Grand Rapids: Zondervan, 1958), p. 8.*

47. Peter Kreeft and Fr. Ronald Taceli, *Handbook of Christian Apologetics (Downers Grove, Ill.: Intervarsity, 1994).*

Chapter Twelve

48. St. Catherine of Siena, *The Dialogue (Mahwah, N.J.: Paulist, 1980), p. 38.*

49. Fr. John Hardon, S.J., *Catholic Dictionary: An Abridged and Updated Edition of Modern Catholic Dictionary* (New York: Random House, 2013), p. 7.

50. For more on the fifteen promises of Mary, visit http://www.fatima.org/essentials/requests/promises.asp.

51. Pope Paul VI, *Mysterium Fidei*, 67.

52. Taken from Pope Leo's Letter to Cardinals di Luca, Pitra, and Hergenroether, *The Catholic Historical Review, vol. 6 (Washington, D.C.: Catholic University of America Press, 1921), p. 5.*

53. Adapted from http://www.rcan.org/index.cfm/fuseaction/feature. display/feature_id/882/index.cfm.

Chapter Fifteen

54. Pope Paul VI, *Sacrosanctum Concilium 8. http://www.ewtn.com/ library/councils/v2litur.htm.*

55. St. Catherine of Siena, "What Leads to Understanding," Meditation of the Day, *Magnificat*, February 15, 2011.

56. http://www.thereligionofpeace.com/Pages/Jesus-Muhammad.htm.

57. *Troy, directed by Wolfgang Petersen, Warner Brothers, 2004.*

58. Pope Benedict XVI, Urbi et Orbi address, Easter 2009, http:// catholicclimatecovenant.org/catholic-teachings/vatican-messages/.

Chapter Eighteen

59. John Paul II, Universal Prayer for Day of Pardon, http://www. vatican.va/holy_father/john_paul_ii/homilies/documents/ hf_jp-ii_hom_20000312_pardon_en.html.

60. Published anonymously in *The Dayspring, Vol. 10 (1881) by the Unitarian Sunday School Society.*

About the Author

Jesse Romero, a retired veteran of the Los Angeles County Sheriff's Department, has a master's degree in Catholic theology from Franciscan University of Steubenville, Ohio. A bilingual speaker, he specializes in evangelization, youth events, apologetics seminars, conferences, and Bible studies. He serves as the director of religious education at a small but growing parish forty minutes north of Los Angeles.